Founding Editor   LISA BEARNSON

Editor-in-Chief   TRACY WHITE

Senior Writer   RACHEL THOMAE

Senior Editor   VANESSA HOY

Copy Editor   KIM SANDOVAL

Contributing Writers   HEATHER JONES, BRITNEY MELLEN

Editorial Assistants   JOANNIE McBRIDE, LIESL RUSSELL

Creative Director   BRIAN TIPPETTS

Art Director, Special Projects   ERIN BAYLESS

Vice President, Group Publisher   DAVID O'NEIL

CK MEDIA

Library of Congress Control Number: 2007926226
White, Tracy
Creating Keepsakes
"A Leisure Arts Publication"

ISBN-13: 978-1-60140-525-8
ISBN-10: 1-60140-525-1

Scrapbooking + Kids = Fun

I love it all—capturing meaningful moments on film, printing photos on my Epson Stylus Photo 2200 printer, and creating pages that will be passed down for generations to come.

But I have to admit that in the past I sometimes felt a little guilty when it came to the creating process. My children were usually in another room playing Nintendo or watching a movie while I worked in my scraproom. I tried including them but often became frustrated as they pulled out patterned paper, stickers, scissors, stamps, paint and other embellishments, making a big mess. They'd try to clean it up—which usually resulted in a bigger mess!

A few years ago, I got smart and set some ground rules for scrapbooking with my kids. The result is quality time in the scraproom for all of us. Here are some of my top tips:

1. Give your kids a few choices of products they can use rather than opening up the entire room.

2. Purchase premade kits—your kids will just have to add photos. I purchased the layout Brecken created here from a scrapbook store. She had a ball putting her own spin on it.

3. Allow your kids to do their own thing. Remember, these are their pages and they don't have to be perfect.

4. Give your kids duplicate photos to scrapbook. If they want to chop off an arm in a photo, it's okay. You still have the original.

5. Always have your kids use their own handwriting for journaling.

6. Write the date the page was created and the child's name on the back of each layout.

7. Put together a stash of supplies your kids can use at any time. I have several Cropper Hopper storage tubs full of decorative-edge scissors, stamps and punches just for my kids.

My friend, Gladys Hedaya, recently shared with me her son's layout, "David's Prehistoric Friends," featured here. Gladys created the layout with David, so he could understand how meaningful scrapbooking is to her. Gladys knew a dinosaur page would pique his interest.

David ate up the one-on-one time with his mom and loved choosing all the embellishments and papers. He stamped, sprinkled embossing powder and held the heat gun. He sketched the dinosaur pictures and wrote about why he loves dinosaurs. Best of all, David felt a boost of confidence when they finished the layout. He and his mom had captured a memory of David's passion for dinosaurs, but more importantly, they had created a wonderful memory together.

Enjoy all the terrific suggestions in *Scrapbooking with Your Kids*. And remember, life's short. Eat chocolate (or even sour gummy worms!) while you're preserving those precious memories with your kids.

Lisa Bearnson

SCRAPBOOKING WITH YOUR kids

THE ULTIMATE GUIDE TO KID-FRIENDLY CRAFTING

A LEISURE ARTS PUBLICATION

LEISURE ARTS
the art of everyday living

Vice President and Editor-in-Chief SANDRA GRAHAM CASE
Executive Director of Publications CHERYL NODINE GUNNELLS
Senior Publications Director SUSAN WHITE SULLIVAN
Special Projects Director SUSAN FRANTZ WILES
Director of Designer Relations DEBRA NETTLES
Senior Prepress Director MARK HAWKINS
Publishing Systems Administrator BECKY RIDDLE
Publishing Systems Assistants CLINT HANSON, JOHN ROSE, KEIJI YUMOTO,
AND LESLEY ANDREWS

Vice President and Chief Operations Officer TOM SIEBENMORGEN
Director of Corporate Planning and Development LATICIA MULL DITTRICH
Vice President, Sales and Marketing PAM STEBBINS
Director of Sales and Services MARGARET REINOLD
Vice President, Operations JIM DITTRICH
Comptroller, Operations ROB THIEME
Retail Customer Service Manager STAN RAYNOR
Print Production Manager FRED F. PRUSS

My Sister

by Brecken and Lisa Bearnson.

David's Prehistoric Friends

by Gladys and David Hedeya.

contents

"every child is an artist"

Can you think of your first art-related memory? Perhaps as a toddler you discovered the power at your fingertips in one simple tool—a crayon! Can you remember how proud you felt when your mother displayed your prized finger-painting—the one you brought home from school—on the refrigerator door for all to see?

You were likely an artist in training before you could even talk! Yet like so many, time goes on and before you know it, it's been years since you've even picked up a crayon. After all, it was Pablo Picasso himself who once said, "Every child is an artist. The problem is how to remain one once he grows up."

As a grown-up scrapbooker or crafter, you've succeeded in harnessing that creative spirit that children seem to inherently possess. And now with children of your own, you get the chance to cultivate that spirit and help it flourish in their lives, too.

The following pages are brimming with scrapbooking-related activities that will fill your home with a love for imaginative exploration. Together, you'll enjoy:

· **Reminiscing over favorite memories.**
· **Discussing family history, including relatives that live both near and far.**
· **Sharing and discussing values.**
· **Getting a little bit messy!**
· **And so much more!**

Remember, as you help your little ones discover their artistic talents, you're sure to learn a thing or two from them, too. It was also Picasso who said, "It took me four years to paint like Raphael, but a lifetime to paint like a child."

Enjoy!

introduction

A majority of the projects in this book can be created using the following supplies. You'll find them in craft, discount or office-supply stores; in the classroom; or even at home.

Adhesive

Glue stick

Craft glue

Papers

Cardstock

Patterned paper

Construction paper

Plain white paper (printer paper)

Envelopes

Coloring Media

Colored pencils

Markers

Crayons

Paint and paint brushes

Felt-tipped pens

Decorating Chalks

Tools

Child-safe scissors (both plain scissors and decorative-edge scissors)

Paper trimmer (to be used by an adult only, etc.)

Shaped punches (heart, star, circle)

Stapler

Hole punch

Fun Extras

Stickers

Ribbons, yarn, string

Flowers

Brads

Rubber stamps and inkpads

Glitter and/or glitter glue

Beads

chapter 1

summer

From *sun* up to sun down, *kids* will *warm* *right* up to these *productive* pastimes!

project 1

by Wendy Sue Anderson

Keep *cool*—capture *memories* of a frozen summer *treat*!

You Will Need: Cardstock, patterned paper, letter stickers, star accents, circle punch, pen

Kid-Friendly: Have your child create a title with letter stickers.

Variation

Substitute a star accent for the word "star" on this cute greeting card.

Try This: Create a story using leftover word and picture stickers.

1

step-by-step:
Position Letter Stickers

1. Choose several styles of letter stickers.

2. Spell out the words, using a ruler to position your stickers.

3. Lay the ruler down on the page and press the stickers off the ruler.

2

3

project 2

by Jessie Baldwin

Make a *splash* with a *pool-party* layout!

You Will Need: Cardstock, ribbon, letter stickers, hole punch, pen
"I liked adding the ribbon. It was like sewing." —VIOLET B., age 6

Variation

Punch holes around the outside of a card and thread with ribbon.

Try This: Thread the card with embroidery floss, raffia, yarn or string.

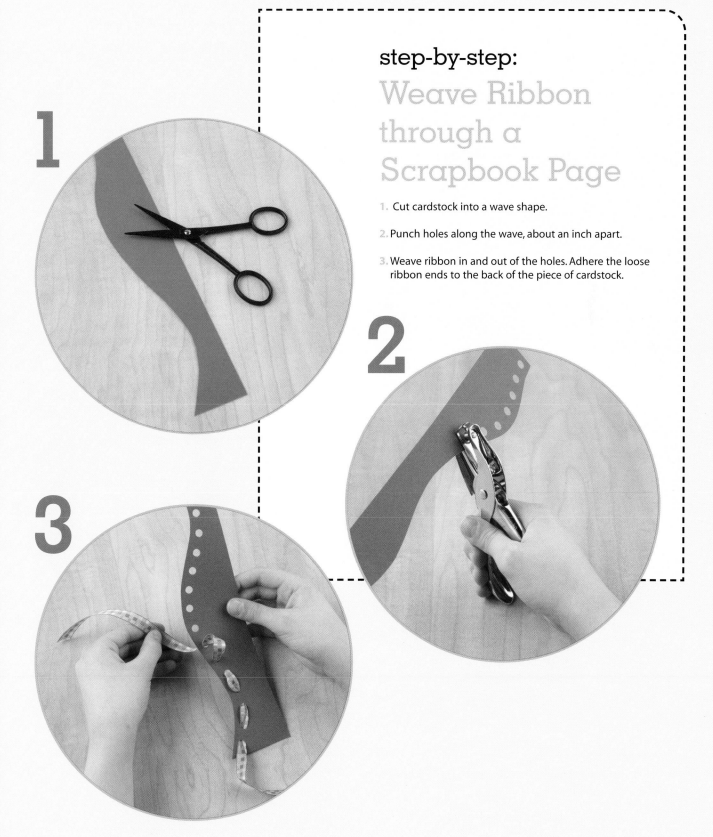

1

step-by-step:

Weave Ribbon through a Scrapbook Page

1. Cut cardstock into a wave shape.

2. Punch holes along the wave, about an inch apart.

3. Weave ribbon in and out of the holes. Adhere the loose ribbon ends to the back of the piece of cardstock.

2

3

project 3

by Linda Harrison

Round up an *assortment* of your *favorite* summer *memories*.

You Will Need: Cardstock, patterned paper, letter stickers, month stickers, star and circle punches

"I really liked making the circles pretty. I liked gluing the shapes."
—LEAH W., age 5

Variation

Make a matching card with your extra scrapbook supplies!

Try This: Make a page or a card with punched square shapes.

1

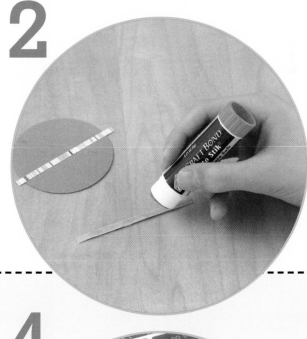

step-by-step:
Create Decorative Circle Accents

1. Punch a circle from cardstock with a large circle punch.

2. Cut thin strips of patterned paper. Glue them on the circle so they make a criss-cross pattern.

3. Punch a star from another color of cardstock. Glue onto the circle.

4. Add a "month" sticker to the circle.

2

3

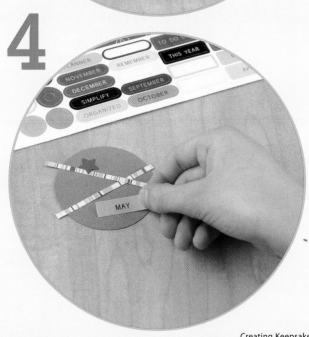

4

project 4

by Denine Zielinski

Let your summer *photographs* *shine* in this *flip-up* mini book.

You Will Need: Chipboard, cardstock, patterned paper, ribbon, letter and number stickers, sun and other decorative stickers, hole punch

"I like the sun sticker for the number '0' in '2006'." —JAEME T., age 8

Look inside!

Attach photographs to the pages, then embellish with stickers.

Try This: Make a flip-up book full of your favorite drawings.

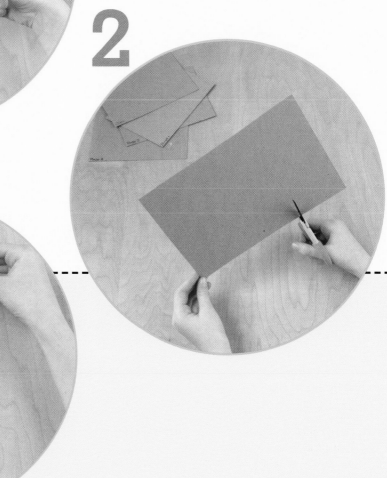

1

step-by-step:
Mini-Book Cover

1. Cut a piece of thin chipboard to 4½" x 6". This will be your cover.

2. Using your cover as a guide, cut a second piece of chipboard. This piece should be ¼" longer than the cover. Continue to cut three more pieces of chipboard. Each piece should be ¼" longer than the previous piece.

3. Stack the chipboard pieces together and embellish as desired.

2

3

project 5

by Wendy Sue Anderson

Save your *best* gift for *Dad*—a *coupon book* he can use year-round!

You Will Need: Cardstock, envelopes, patterned paper, letter stickers, ribbon, "Dad" sticker, hole punch, hole reinforcements

"Dad's gonna love this! Maybe you can make one for ME for my birthday!"
—JOSHUA A., age 10

Look inside!

Embellish your pages with leftover stickers and paper scraps. Tuck notes inside the envelopes if desired.

Just for Fun: Make a coupon book to give to your favorite teacher!

1

step-by-step:
Coupon Book

1. Make a list of the things you want to do for your dad.

2. On the computer, create serveral coupons. Cut them out.

3. Glue patterned paper and a coupon onto the front of each envelope.

4. Punch holes and place hole reinforcements at the top of each page. Bind together with ribbon.

2

3

4

by Denine Zielinski

Smile! This cute *chore chart* will make your *jobs* fun!

You Will Need: Whiteboard, letter and picture stickers, pen, thin black tape, circle punch, smiley-face stamp, inkpad, magnets, contact paper

Kid-Friendly: Have your child choose stickers for the chore categories and make smiley-face magnets for the chore chart.

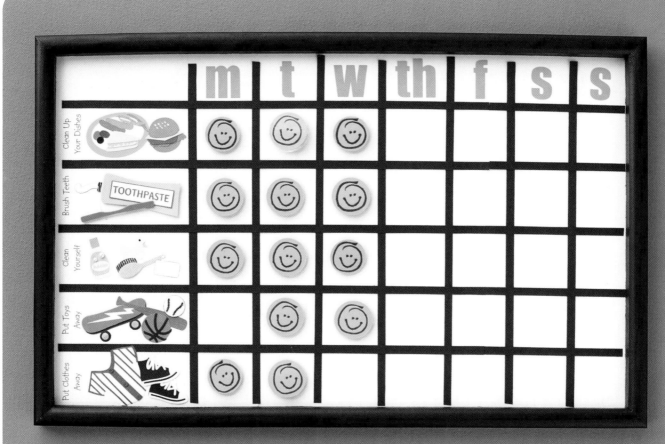

Variation

Go to the head of the class with this handy homework chart!

Try This: Make a chart of your goals for the summer and mark each one as you accomplish it.

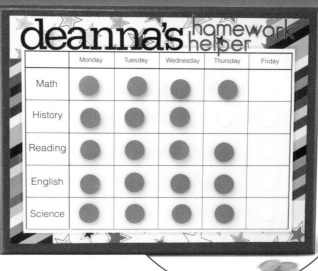

1

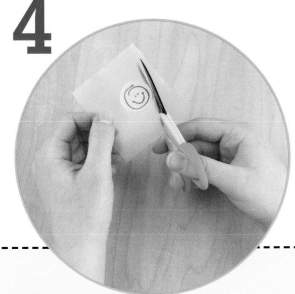

step-by-step:
Smiley-Face Chore Chart Magnets

1. Stamp a smiley face on cardstock.

2. Use a circle punch to punch out the smiley face.

3. Place the punched smiley face face-down on contact paper. Fold the contact paper to cover both sides of the smiley face.

4. Cut around the contact paper.

5. Adhere a small magnet to the back of each smiley face.

2

4

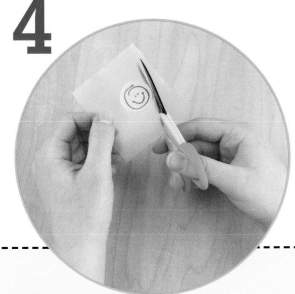

3

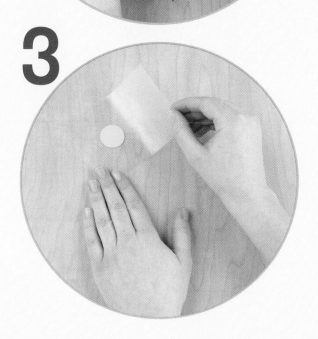

5

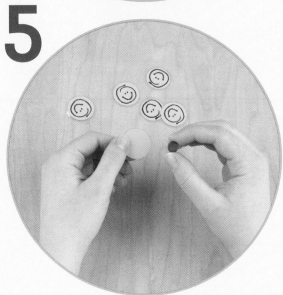

project 7

by Linda Harrison

Design your own license to ride!

You Will Need: Cardstock, letter stickers, pen, ribbon, star punch, hole punch

Kid-Friendly: Have your child trace the tags onto cardstock, then cut them out with child-safe scissors.

Note: Consider laminating the decorated tag for extra protection.

Variation

Customize tags with your name or with clever sayings.

Try This: Celebrate the summer by creating bike tags for all of your friends. Decorate your bikes and have a parade!

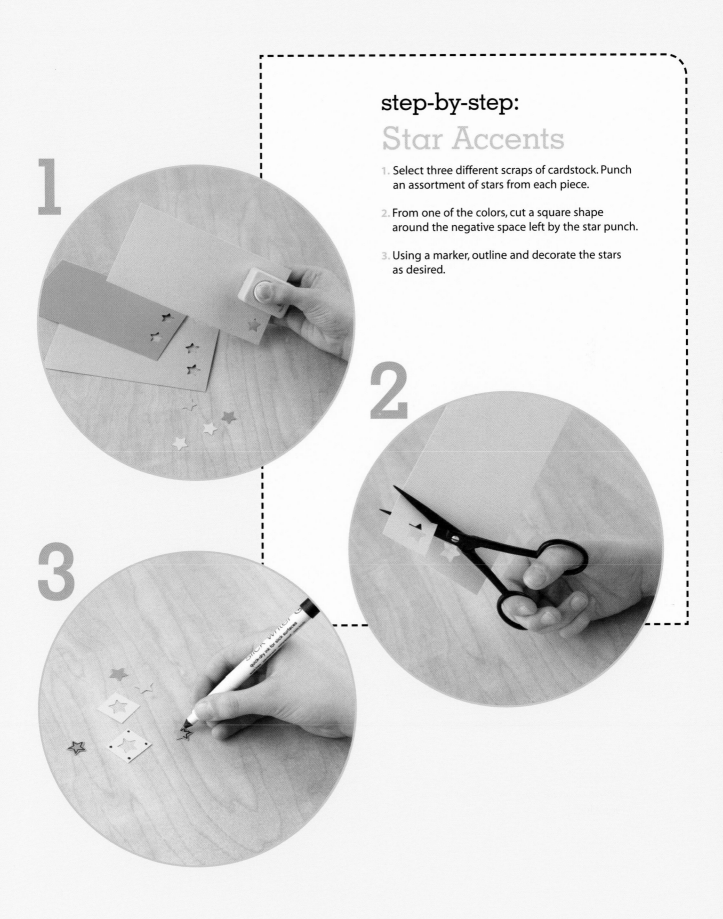

step-by-step:
Star Accents

1. Select three different scraps of cardstock. Punch an assortment of stars from each piece.

2. From one of the colors, cut a square shape around the negative space left by the star punch.

3. Using a marker, outline and decorate the stars as desired.

project 8

by Denine Zielinski

Pocket your favorite *travel* memories in this *take-along* travel companion.

You Will Need: Cardstock, patterned paper, ribbon, letter stickers, mini clipboard, hole punch

"The clipboard is awesome. I would use it to make notes in the car when my mom was driving." —JAEME T., age 8

Variation!

Draw or print out games (such as tic tac toe) and clip them to this board.

Try This: Create an "outdoor adventure" book and use it to keep track of the bugs, birds and animals you spot in your neighborhood this summer.

1

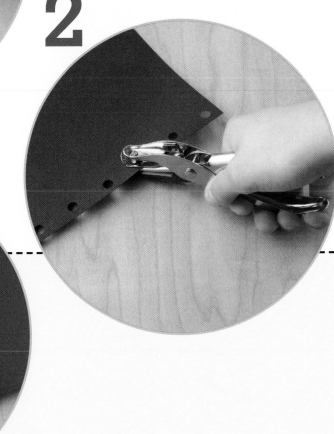

step-by-step:
Travel Pocket

1. Start with two sheets of 8½" x 11" cardstock. Use a ruler to mark holes on one piece of cardstock, about 1" apart.

2. Holding both pieces of cardstock together, punch holes with a hole punch.

3. Tie a knot at the end of about 4' of ribbon. Weave the opposite end through the punched holes to hold the paper together. Tie a knot after the last hole.

2

3

project 9

by Wendy Sue Anderson

Enjoy a *summer* full of *adventures* with this cool *passport*.

You Will Need: Cardstock, envelopes, patterned paper, die cuts, number and picture stickers, ribbon, circle punch, hole punch, binder ring

Kid-Friendly: Let your child help choose the activities and decorate each passport page.

2007
{summer}
fun
passport

25

fun
things
to do this summer

{ice cream}

Is today a good day for ice cream? You can choose what kind of ice cream and we'll have a yummy treat!

Look inside!

Add a stamp or a sticker to each completed passport activity. If desired, tuck notes inside the envelopes.

Try This: Make a passport for every season of the year!

1

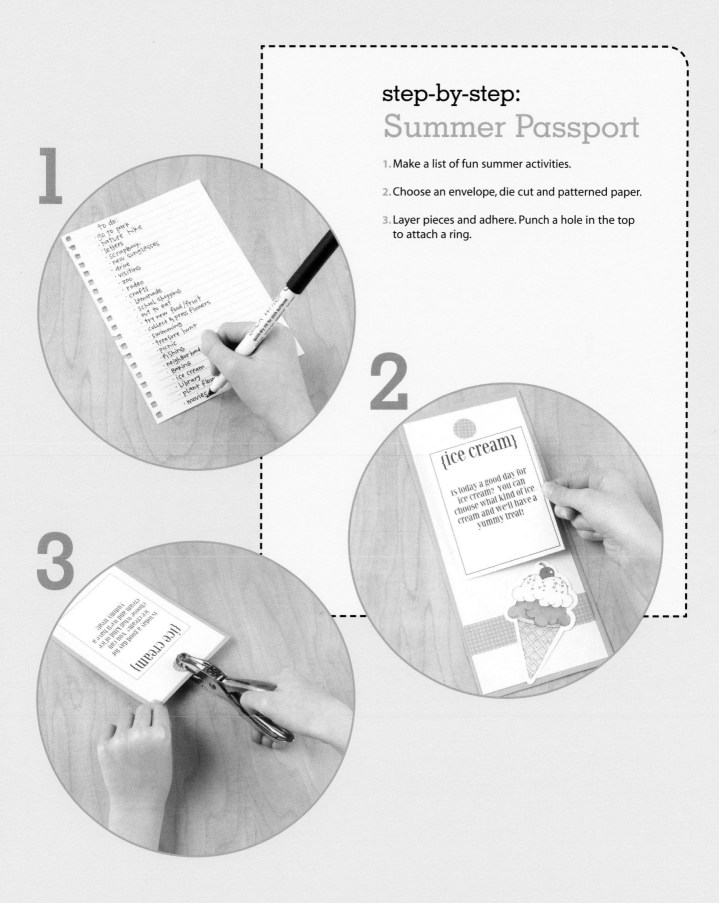

step-by-step:
Summer Passport

1. Make a list of fun summer activities.

2. Choose an envelope, die cut and patterned paper.

3. Layer pieces and adhere. Punch a hole in the top to attach a ring.

2

3

to do:
- go to park
- nature hike
- letters
- scrapbook
- new sunglasses
- drive
- visiting
- zoo
- rodeo
- crafts
- lemonade
- school shopping
- out to eat
- try new food/fruit
- collect & press flowers
- swimming
- treasure hunt
- picnic
- fishing
- neighborhood
- baking
- ice cream
- library
- plant flowers
- movies

{ice cream}

Is today a good day for ice cream? you can choose what kind of ice cream and we'll have a yummy treat!

project 10

by Cindy Knowles

Choose to have a *fun* summer with this *jar* full of *activities*.

You Will Need: Empty jar, patterned paper, letter and sun stickers, ribbon, tag

"Oh, I love this! Whenever I get bored, I can always choose an activity!" —JAEME T., age 8

Variation

Create a family gratitude jar—write thank-you notes to each other and read them aloud once a month.

Try This: Photograph your family participating in summer activities and then scrapbook the pictures!

1

step-by-step:

Summer-Fun Jar

1. Adhere a strip of patterned paper around a jar.

2. Create a tag and add the words "Summer Fun."

3. Tie a ribbon around the top of the jar. Add the tag to the ribbon.

4. Write a list of summer activities. Cut them into individual strips, fold each strip in half and place inside the jar.

2

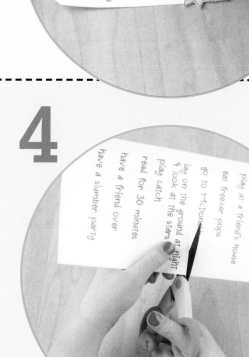

3

4

project 11

by Erin Lincoln

Stay on *track* for *summertime* with this *custom-made* clock.

You Will Need: Plastic clock, patterned paper, cardstock, letter and number stickers, flower punch, buttons

Kid-Friendly: Have your child add word or picture stickers to the clock face.

Variation

Here's another take on a clock that's fun to make!

Try This: If you have a pet create a schedule to remind you when it's time to play, walk, nap, eat and practice tricks!

1

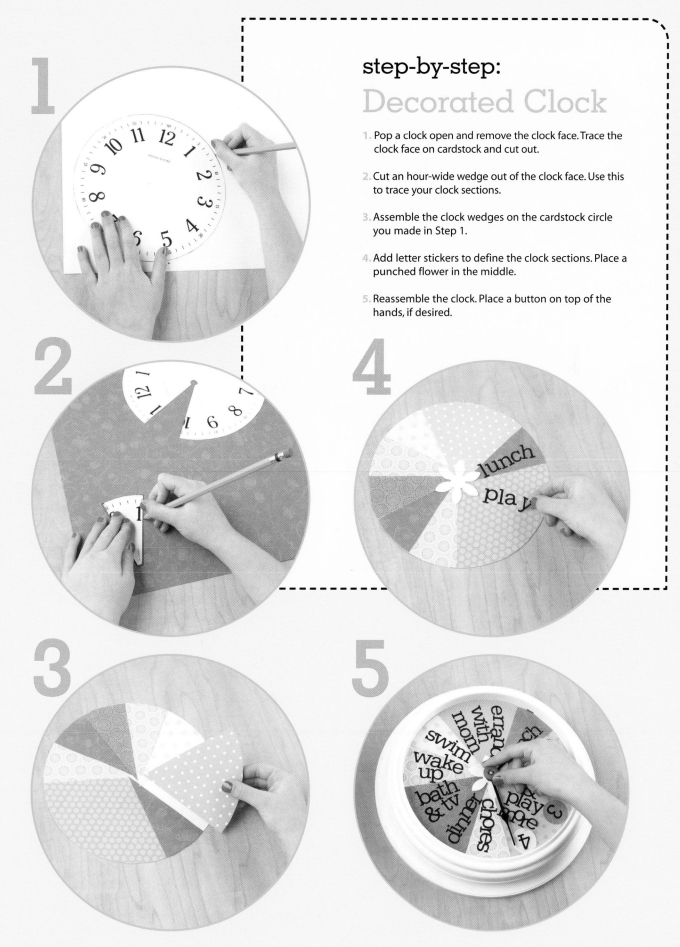

step-by-step:
Decorated Clock

1. Pop a clock open and remove the clock face. Trace the clock face on cardstock and cut out.

2. Cut an hour-wide wedge out of the clock face. Use this to trace your clock sections.

3. Assemble the clock wedges on the cardstock circle you made in Step 1.

4. Add letter stickers to define the clock sections. Place a punched flower in the middle.

5. Reassemble the clock. Place a button on top of the hands, if desired.

2

4

3

5

article

How can I *best* set up a child's *crafting* area and
organize my child's *art supplies*?

A well-stocked, organized crafting space is the first step in helping a child explore his or her creativity. Whether you choose to set up shop in a corner of the dining room or you have an entire room to dedicate to the cause, here are five tips to get you (and your little Van Gogh) creating in no time!

- **Add a roll of butcher paper** to a towel holder or dowel and attach it to the end of the table for a renewable, mess-free crafting/coloring surface. (Opposite)

- **Store similar supplies** in labeled baskets or bins. Paint a small piece of plywood with chalkboard paint to create labels that you can change as you swap out supplies. (Right)

- **Lightweight buckets** full of supplies are easy for children to tote to and from the crafting area. Hang labeled buckets on a wall-mounted peg-board to keep crafting surfaces free of clutter. (Bottom)

- **Shoeboxes** are an inexpensive solution for dividing and storing art supplies. As a bonus project, let children decorate and label them with the appropriate supplies (for example, use paint to decorate boxes of paint, crayons for boxes of crayons, etc.).

- **Take advantage of** back-to-school sales in the late summer to stock up on children's art supplies. Fill a large plastic bin with overflow supplies so you don't accidentally run out of glue sticks or construction paper mid-project!

Cowboy party Set

"I *like* this party set! I think it's really cute! I *want to* take the *checkerboard* home with me. Can I?" —KAYLEE M., AGE 8

You're Invited to ...
a Cowboy Party!

by Joannie McBride

Round up your friends for a backyard barbecue this summer. Start with your own personalized brand of invitations and add western flair with party favors and decorations.

COME ON OVER
PARTNER!

WHEN: SATURDAY, AUGUST 2

WHERE: OVER AT WYATT'S PLACE

TIME: 2:00 P.M.

PLEASE R.S.V.P.

SEE YA THERE BUCK-A-ROO!

school

Provide *children* with a *retreat* from busy *schoolwork*, or help them take on *school* projects with an *artistic* attitude.

Here's a *scrapbook* page that *makes* the *grade!*

You Will Need: Cardstock, patterned paper, ribbon, letter stickers, pen, inkpad, corner-rounder punch, paper clip

Kid-Friendly: Have your child write names and dates on strips of paper, and trim the ribbons.

Variation

Do the math—use numbers to help create a greeting for a great math teacher.

Try This: Spell out greetings with number stickers.

1

step-by-step:

Inking Embellishments

1. Trim a narrow piece of paper. Have your child write words on the paper.

2. Snip the paper into shorter strips.

3. Saturate the paper edges with an inkpad. Allow each strip to dry for a couple of minutes before adhering it to the layout.

2

3

Put your *school* memories in *shape* *with* this easy page *solution*!

You Will Need: Cardstock, patterned paper, chipboard letters, letter stamps, inkpad, pen

Kid-Friendly: Have your child add handwritten notes and mat the photos on cardstock.

SCHOOL DAYS

Name
Tanner Knowles

School
Oak Grove

Teacher
Mrs. Darlington

Grade
1st grade

Friends
Darin, Jason, and Dustin

Fav Subject
Writing

Variation

Got extra page supplies? Make a cute card!

Try This: Challenge yourself to make as many cards and gift tags as you can from three pieces of cardstock, three pieces of patterned paper and a sheet of letter stickers.

1

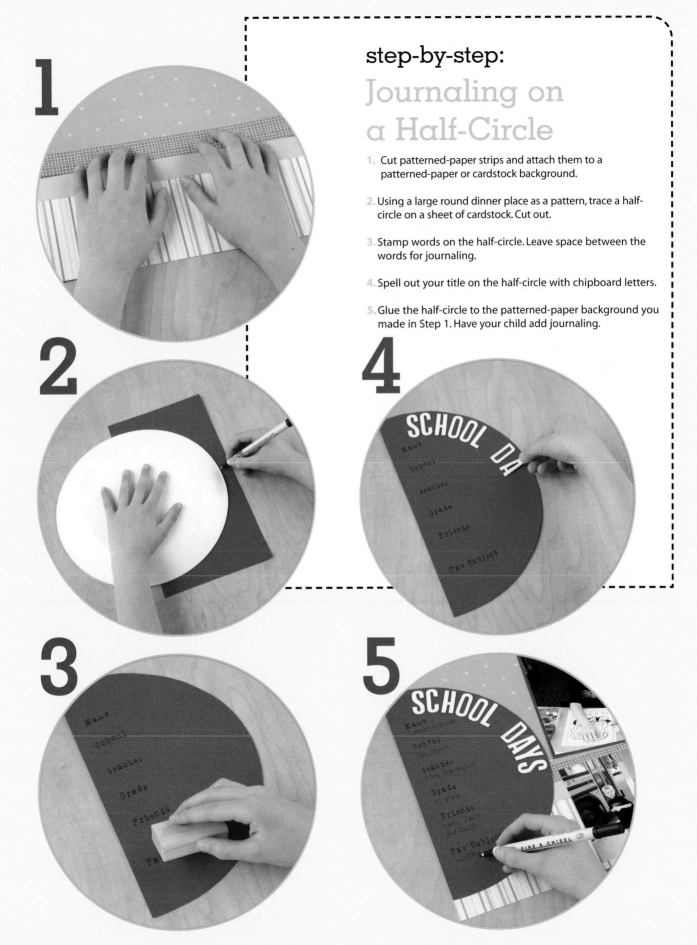

step-by-step:
Journaling on a Half-Circle

1. Cut patterned-paper strips and attach them to a patterned-paper or cardstock background.

2. Using a large round dinner place as a pattern, trace a half-circle on a sheet of cardstock. Cut out.

3. Stamp words on the half-circle. Leave space between the words for journaling.

4. Spell out your title on the half-circle with chipboard letters.

5. Glue the half-circle to the patterned-paper background you made in Step 1. Have your child add journaling.

2

4

3

5

project 3

by Heather Preckel

Let your *favorite* teacher be the *star* of your next *scrapbook* page!

You Will Need: Cardstock, patterned paper, letter stickers, pen, star punch, colored pencil

"I like having a page of my own for my favorite teacher!"
—KIERSTEN P., age 7

my
FAVORITE
teacher

Mr. Allison - Kindergarten '04

to my
TEACHER

Variation

Design a card around a star theme for a favorite teacher!

Try This: Use a star-shaped punch to create a card for someone you love.

1

step-by-step:
Punched Border Strip

1. Cut two orange strips and two white strips.

2. Punch stars from the white strip.

3. Layer the white strip over the orange strip. Adhere.

4. Draw a border on the top and bottom of the finished star strip.

2

3

4

project 4

by Nisa Fiin

It's as *easy* as ABC to *create* a mini *gift* album for a *teacher*!

You Will Need: Blank book or mini album to decorate, patterned paper, ribbon, letter stamps, inkpad, star punch, hole punch

Kid-Friendly: Have your child stamp "Thank You" on the front cover and select her favorite photos to include on the inside pages.

Look inside!

Handwrite sentiments on the inside pages of the book.

Try This: Ask each student in the classroom to submit one picture. Compile them into an album for a year-end teacher's thank-you gift.

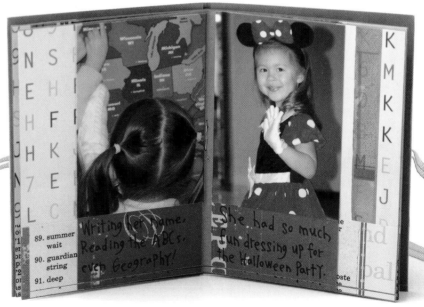

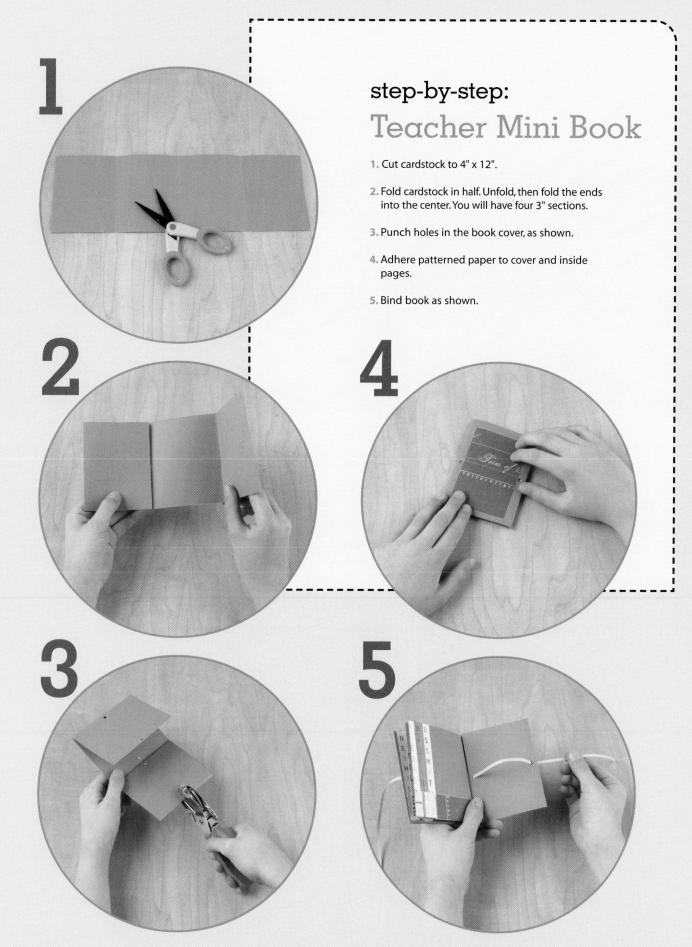

1

2

3

step-by-step:
Teacher Mini Book

1. Cut cardstock to 4" x 12".

2. Fold cardstock in half. Unfold, then fold the ends into the center. You will have four 3" sections.

3. Punch holes in the book cover, as shown.

4. Adhere patterned paper to cover and inside pages.

5. Bind book as shown.

4

5

project 5

by Wendy Sue Anderson

Make your *mark* with these *adorable* triangular *bookmarks*.

You Will Need: Envelope, patterned paper, flower punch, button

"This is fun! I want to make a different one for every one of my books!"
—SETH A., age 3

Variation

Design a collection of bookmarks for your entire library.

Try This: Giving a book for a gift? Add a cute bookmark to make the gift complete!

1

step-by-step:
Envelope Corner Bookmark

1. Measure each side of the envelope to create a perfect triangular corner.

2. Cut off the corner with a paper trimmer or scissors.

3. Add patterned paper, a flower punch and a button.

4. Slip the bookmark onto a corner of a page in your book to save your place.

2

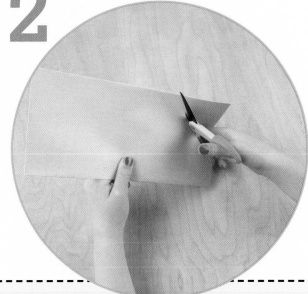

3

4

project 6
by Wendy Sue Anderson

Trace your way *through* your family *history*.

You Will Need: Cardstock, patterned paper, binder rings, ribbon, hole punch, lamination, dry-erase marker

"I like having this book with me at church." —SETH A., age 3

Look inside!
Use a dry-erase marker to trace the words in your book.

Try This: Make an ABC tracing book.

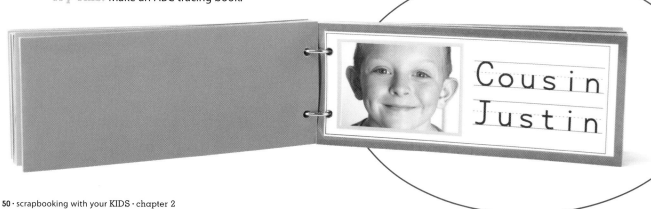

1

2

step-by-step:
Family Tracing Book

1. Choose and print the photographs you want to use for your project.

2. Type the names or words you want to put in your book and print.

3. Mat photos and text on colored cardstock.

4. Laminate the pages after they're complete. Assemble the book by punching holes and attaching the pages with binder rings.

Brother
Josh

3

Brother
sh

4

Br

project 7

by Denine Zielinski

Schoolwork is fun with these cute flashcards!

You Will Need: Cardstock, letter and picture stickers, hole punch, corner-rounder punch, pen, binder ring

"I liked being able to make these cards to practice my words for school." —DEVIN T., age 6

Variation

Make a set of number flashcards.

Try This: Laminate cards for extra durability.

1

step-by-step:
Alphabet Cards

1. Cut cardstock into colored and white rectangles as shown. Round the edges.

2. Attach white cardstock to colored cardstock.

3. Add letter stickers and picture stickers.

4. Write words on white cardstock and cut them out. Adhere to the back of the cards.

2

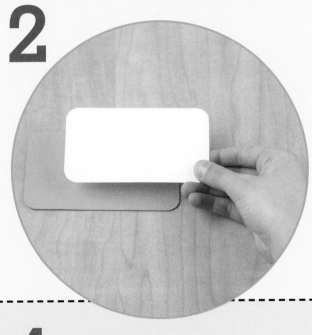

3

4

project 8

by Cindy Knowles

Turn your *leftover stickers* into a *fun* bingo game!

You Will Need: Cardstock, stickers, pen

"My brothers and sisters kept coming over and saying, 'I want to do that, too!'"—CALEB K., age 6

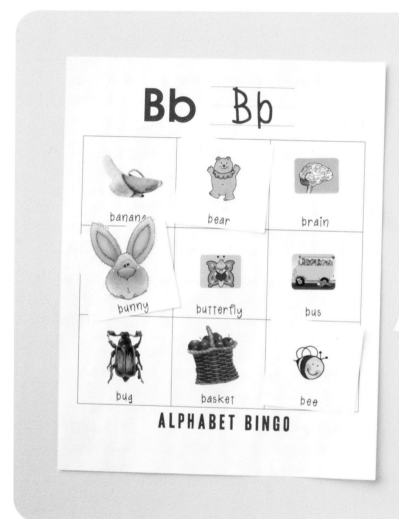

Variation

Use candy, coins, buttons or other small objects as markers for your bingo game.

Try This: Make a math or social studies bingo game using facts from your child's school work.

1

1. Draw a nine-box bingo board by hand or on your computer. Add one letter of the alphabet to the top of each page. Print two copies.

2. Place one sticker in each square of both bingo boards.

3. With a fine-point marker, write the name of the object below the sticker.

4. Cut one board apart. These will be your bingo calling cards.

2

3

4

project 9

by Joannie McBride

Jumpstart your *journaling* with *prompts* from this cute *jar!*

You Will Need: Jar, patterned paper, ribbon, tags

"I love writing about these topics!" —ASHLEY L., age 12

My favorite pastime?

Variation

Decorate your jar with colors to match your room.

Try This: Use favorite quotes or movie titles as journaling prompts.

1

step-by-step:

Decorated
Journaling Jar

1. Cut patterned paper to the size of the jar.

2. Adhere the patterned paper to the jar.

3. Add ribbon and other embellishments as desired.

2

3

Tuck special *notes* to family *members* inside this *adorable* mail *sorter*.

You Will Need: Mail sorter, cardstock, patterned paper, hole punch, corner-rounder punch, ribbon, letter stickers, paper clips

"I can't wait to get a letter!" —RYAN W., age 7

Variation

Create a family message board.

Try This: Pin a photo on your message board and ask each family member to jot down a word or two about the photo. Use the words for journaling on a scrapbook page.

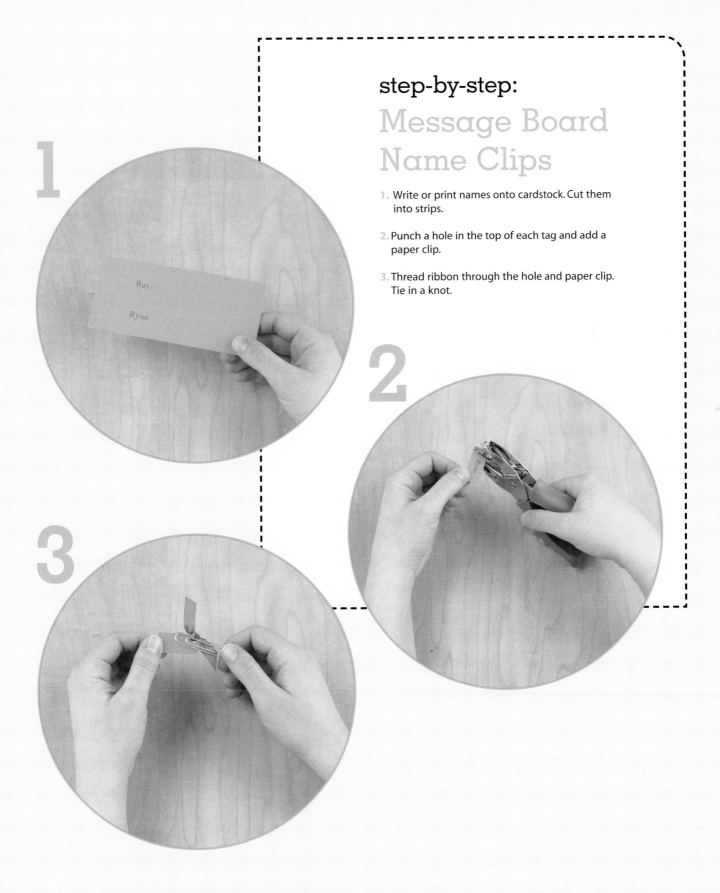

1

step-by-step:

Message Board
Name Clips

1. Write or print names onto cardstock. Cut them into strips.

2. Punch a hole in the top of each tag and add a paper clip.

3. Thread ribbon through the hole and paper clip. Tie in a knot.

2

3

project 11

by Erin Lincoln

Display your child's artwork in a creative way!

You Will Need: Frame, artwork, letter stickers, ribbon, scanner

Kid-Friendly: Ask your child to select his favorite artwork to scan or photograph for this project.

Variation

Another great option for sharing your child's artwork? Place it in a mini album!

Try This: Ask your child for his comments about the items he's created and record them on the pages of his mini book.

1

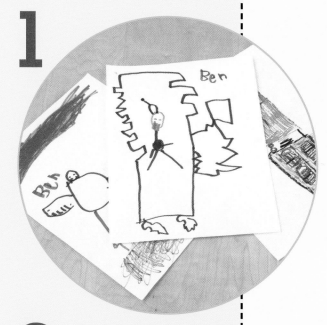

1. Scan artwork into your computer and resize each picture to 3" x 2¼".

2. Print and assemble on a piece of cardstock for backing. Trim the cardstock around the pictures to make a strip.

3. Place ribbon across the top of the strip to create a border.

4. Place in a frame over another piece of artwork. Use letter stickers to create a title piece on top of the glass.

2

3

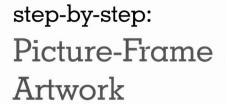

4

article

How can I best *display* my child's *artwork*?

What child doesn't beam with pride over a personal creation displayed on the refrigerator door for everyone to admire? A fine solution indeed, but don't stop there! Give the fridge a rest and try the following five ideas:

- **Showcase current works of art** on a clothesline adorned with old-fashioned clothespins. It's a charming look—and it will keep your walls hole-free! (Bottom)

- **Scan or photograph artwork** to incorporate onto a scrapbook page showing each year's favorite masterpieces. (Below)

- **Reduce artwork** (with a scanner or copier) and print 4" x 6" copies to include in a "brag book" to display on a coffee table or desk.

- **Scan artwork** and use the digital images to create a slideshow screen saver for the family computer. (Opposite)

- **Go all out** and dedicate one wall in your home as the family "gallery." Choose frames that allow artwork to be easily swapped out each month, and be sure to equip the area with good lighting.

Chinese New Year party Set

The Year of the Ox 1913, 1925, 1937, 1949, 1961, 1973, 1985, 1997

People born in the Year of the Ox are patient, speak little, and inspire confidence in others. They tend, however, to be eccentric, and bigoted, and they anger easily. They have fierce tempers and although they speak little, when they do they are quite eloquent. Ox people are mentally and physically alert. Generally easy-going, they can be remarkably stubborn, and they hate to fail or be opposed. They are most compatible with Snake, Rooster, and Rat people.

"Mom, when can we have this party?" —DAVID R., AGE 9

You're Invited to a ... Chinese New Year Party!

by Gail Robinson

No matter what year your party guests were born, they'll enjoy good fortune (and learn a little bit of history at the same time!) when they ring in the Chinese New Year with this fun party theme.

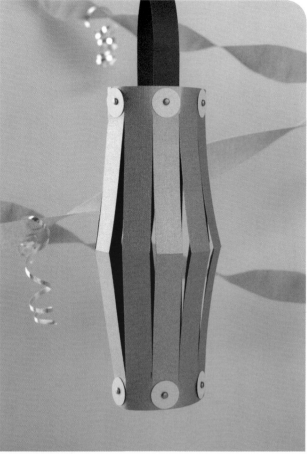

Happy New Year!

Please join our class
for welcoming in
"The Year of the Pig"

February 19, 2007
1:00 p.m.
Mrs. Brown's classroom

"Gung hay fat choy!"

gifts

Little ones will beam at the prospect of giving (or receiving) a one-of-a-kind original (just like them!).

project 1

by Cindy Knowles

Here's a cool *solution* for *framing* your *friends*!

You Will Need: Photo frames, ribbon, letter stickers, flower die cuts, tags, pen

"I used pictures of me and made a gift for my dad." —EMILIA E., age 11

Variation

Pass notes in style with this cute card.

Try This: Decorate a card with hearts for a Valentine's Day gift.

step-by-step:
Accordion Photo Display

1. Center and attach photos to the back of each frame.

2. Cover the back of each frame with patterned paper.

3. Punch holes in the frames as shown.

4. Tie together with ribbon. Add flower die cuts and embellishments to each frame.

1

2

3

4

project 2

by Heather Preckel

You'll *love* this *easy* scrapbook *page*—and so will your *mom* or *dad*!

You Will Need: Cardstock, patterned paper, ribbon, hole punch

"This was just as easy as tying my shoes!" —KIERSTEN P., age 7

YOU ARE THE BEST DADDY IN THE WHOLE WORLD!

Variation

Add a touch of heart to a greeting card for a favorite person.

Try This: Punch several hearts from cardstock and tie them together with ribbon or yarn.

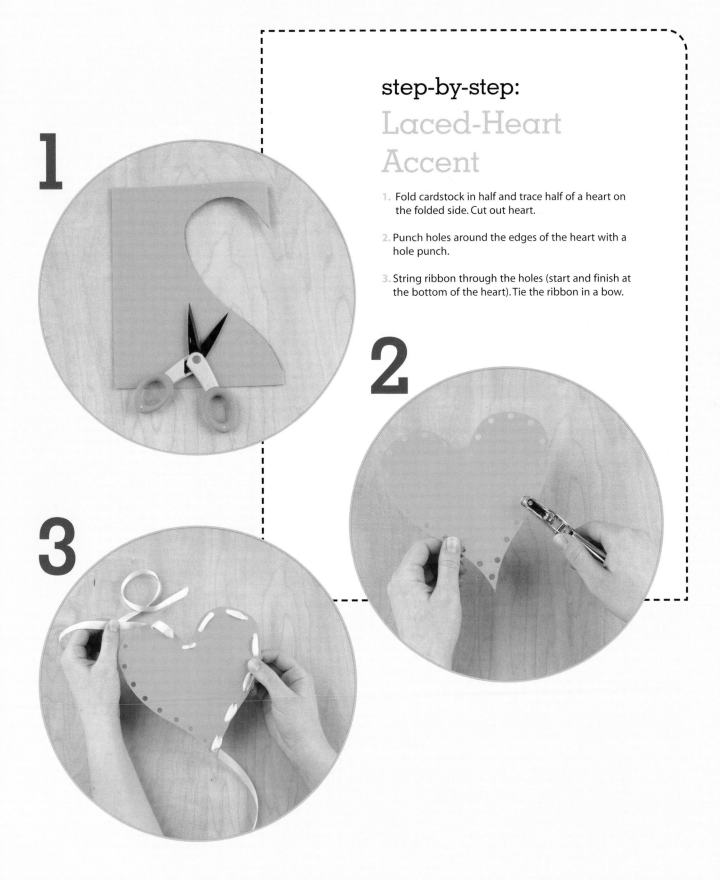

1

step-by-step:

Laced-Heart Accent

1. Fold cardstock in half and trace half of a heart on the folded side. Cut out heart.

2. Punch holes around the edges of the heart with a hole punch.

3. String ribbon through the holes (start and finish at the bottom of the heart). Tie the ribbon in a bow.

2

3

project 3

by Vicki Harvey

Create a *gift* page that *Grandma* will *love*!

You Will Need: Cardstock, patterned paper, rubber stamp, ribbon, pen, letter stickers, inkpad, tag

Kid-Friendly: Have your child handwrite her journaling on the strips of cardstock.

she brings me shoping all of my Birthdays

she is Nice

We Bake cookies Together

I have sleepovers with her

I Love Grahdma

Variation

Make a card extra special with a decorated tag.

Try This: Decorate a handmade card with leftover scraps of patterned paper.

step-by-step:
Gift Layout

1. Attach pink paper to floral background paper. Add a photo.

2. Cut a heart from pink cardstock. Stamp with a "Love" stamp.

3. Attach the pink heart above the photo. Create the title by placing a "U" sticker on a tag tied with green ribbon. Add the "I" sticker as shown.

4. Have your child journal on cardstock strips and attach them to the layout.

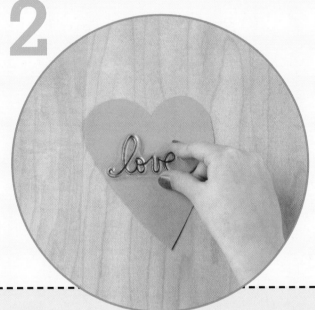

project 4

by Marla Kress

Record your *adventures* in this *fun mini book*!

You Will Need: Mini book, cardstock, patterned paper, letter stickers, small toy

Kid-Friendly: Have your child layer and glue papers onto the book, then add a title with letter stickers.

Look Inside!

Tell your favorite stories on the pages of your mini book!

Try This: Write and illustrate fictional stories inside your book.

step-by-step:
Mini-Book Cover

1. Cut strips of patterned paper to size.

2. Remove the cover from a mini album and attach strips of papers and a photo.

3. Add letter stickers to create the title.

4. Replace the album cover. Journal on the solid strip of paper. Add a toy to the cover.

project 5

by Linda Harrison

Combine *squares* and *triangles* into a *colorful* picture *frame*.

You Will Need: Cardstock, patterned paper, square punch

"I liked to punch out the squares." —ROBBY H., age 4

Variation

Get a whole new look by choosing a different color of paper for your frame.

Try This: Doing this project with a younger child? Larger mosaic pieces will help you finish a bit faster.

step-by-step:
Mosaic Technique

1. To create the mosaic look, punch out multiple squares from your patterned paper.

2. Leave some squares whole. Cut other squares into triangles.

3. Attach the pieces to your frame, starting in one corner and filling the frame as desired.

project 6

by Jessie Baldwin

You'll be on a *roll* when you *use* your *paper* scraps to *make* this picture *frame*!

You Will Need: Cardstock, patterned paper

"It was cool that the paper made triangles when I folded it. I want to put this in my room." —VIOLET B., age 7

Variation

For a variation, try changing the size, shape and colors of your paper rolls.

Try This: Jazz up your frame with paint or glitter.

1

step-by-step:

Rolled-Paper Frame

1. Cut rectangle-shaped strips from patterned paper or cardstock.

2. Fold the rectangles. Fold them over and over on themselves, then open them up so they make a triangle. Glue the strips so they remain folded.

3. Assemble the frame with the various strips. Trim as necessary to make everything fit together.

2

3

project 7

by Cindy Knowles

Make a *note* of it: these *mini* notepads are *fun-and-easy* gifts for *friends*!

You Will Need: Cardstock, patterned paper, sticky-note pad, silk flower, brad

"I liked making this because I got to choose my favorite colors."
—SHERIDAN A., age 5

Variation

Want a different look? Change out your papers and embellishments!

Try This: Add a magnetic strip to the back of the notepad and hang it on your refrigerator.

step-by-step:

Decorative Flower Notepad

1. Glue patterned paper to cardstock or cardboard.

2. Glue a strip of colored cardstock to a strip of white cardstock, centering it from top to bottom.

3. Attach a flower to the cardstock strip with a brad and adhere to the top portion of the patterned-paper background.

4. Glue the cardstock strip and the bottom page of the sticky-note pad to the patterned-paper background.

1

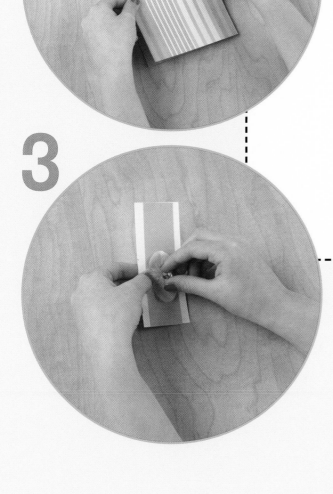

2

3

4

project 8

by Cindy Knowles

For a *picture*-perfect gift, *decorate* a photo cube with *photos* and *embellishments.*

You Will Need: Plastic photo cube, cardstock, letter stickers, stamp and inkpad

"I liked making this as a present for my mom. She is going to be so surprised!" —DOMINIQUE A., age 8

Variation

Customize this gift with colors that will coordinate with the recipient's home.

Try This: Purchase and decorate a plastic frame from your favorite discount store.

step-by-step:
Photo Cube

1. Cut cardstock into a square that is the size of one side of the cube. Use it to trace and trim five photos.

2. Inside the plastic photo cube, you'll find a cardboard cube. Remove the cardboard cube and attach your photos as shown.

3. On one cardstock square, use stickers to spell out the name of the person in the photos.

4. Stamp a fun design on the cardstock square. Attach decorated cardstock square to cardboard cube.

5. Enclose the decorated cardboard cube inside the plastic photo cube.

Keep *Dad's* special treats *close* at *hand* with this *simple* gift!

You Will Need: Can, patterned paper, wooden tag, letter stickers, ribbon, pen

"My daddy will love it that it has his name on it!" —EMILY Z., age 5

Variation

Design your own pencil holder.

Try This: Substitute your own artwork for the patterned paper on this project.

1

step-by-step:
Wooden Tag

1. Trace the outline of the wooden tag onto paper.

2. Cut out the paper tag.

3. Punch a hole in the tag and add a personalized message.

4. Adhere the paper tag to the wooden tag.

5. Lightly sand the edges of the paper on the wooden tag. Run ribbon through the hole and attach to the paper-wrapped can.

2

4

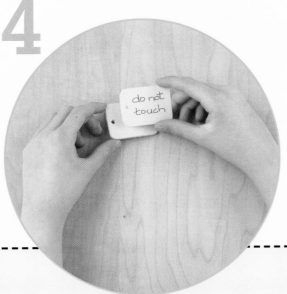

3

5

project 10

by Miriam Campbell

Design a *fashionable* purse *album.*

You Will Need: Inexpensive photo "brag book", cardboard or chipboard, cardstock, patterned paper, beads, wire

"These are so cool—my friends would like getting them as gifts."
—JAEME T., age 8

Variation

Journal in style with this purse notebook.

Try This: Make an assortment of decorated notebooks to match your favorite outfits!

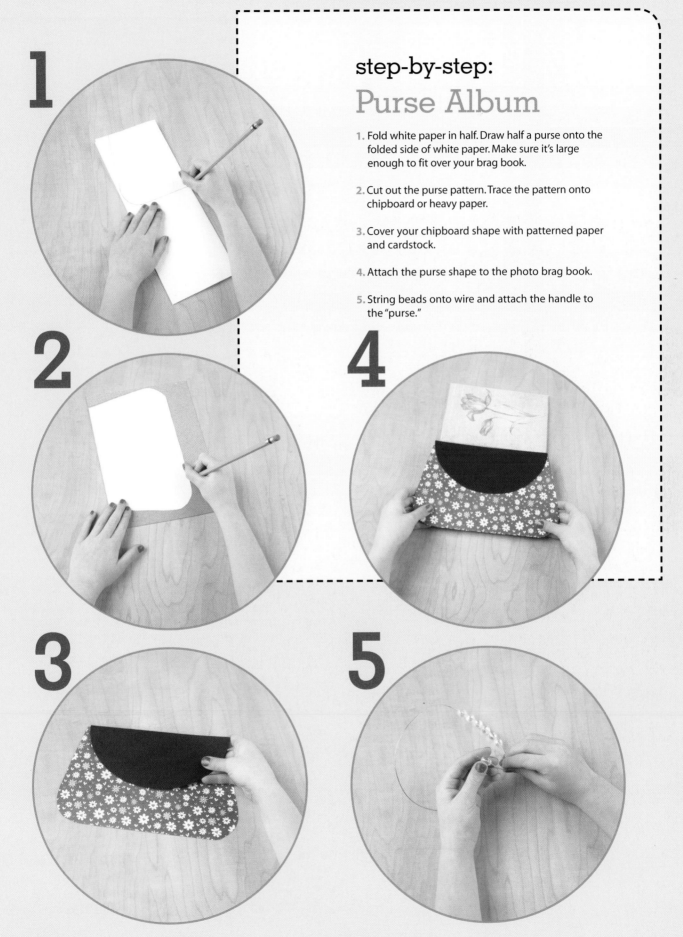

1

step-by-step:
Purse Album

1. Fold white paper in half. Draw half a purse onto the folded side of white paper. Make sure it's large enough to fit over your brag book.

2. Cut out the purse pattern. Trace the pattern onto chipboard or heavy paper.

3. Cover your chipboard shape with patterned paper and cardstock.

4. Attach the purse shape to the photo brag book.

5. String beads onto wire and attach the handle to the "purse."

2

4

3

5

project 11

by Emily Magleby

Brighten someone's day with a *vase* of photo *flowers* in *bloom*!

You Will Need: Vase, shredded paper, cardstock, buttons, circle punch, pipe cleaners, ribbon, thread, tape, pen

Kid-Friendly: Have your child trace and cut out the flower shapes, then add pipe-cleaner stems.

Variation

One perfect felt flower in a bud vase is a great teacher gift!

Try This: Make flowers from patterned-paper scraps and embellishments.

1

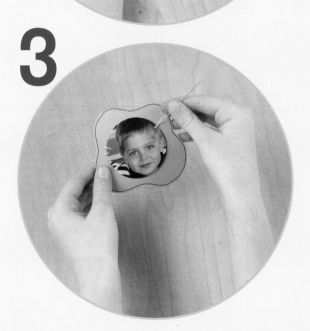

step-by-step:
Photo Flowers

1. Draw five flower shapes onto cardstock. Cut out.

2. Outline the flowers with a black pen. Sew buttons to the middle of four flowers.

3. Use a circle punch to punch out a photo. Stitch photo onto the remaining flower as shown.

4. Tape pipe cleaners to the backs of the flowers.

5. Put the shredded paper in the vase to fill the bottom. Arrange flowers and tie ribbon around the vase.

2

4

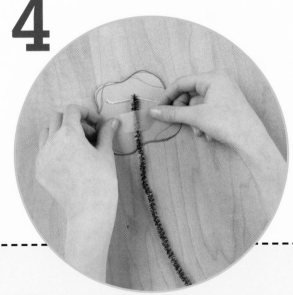

3

5

article

How can my *child* and I *craft* to help *others*?

An ideal parent-child bonding activity, crafting can also build character and foster feelings of compassion in little ones. These ideas will help children learn the value of sharing their artistic talents with others:

- **Show your little one** how to turn a retired finger-painting into a sweet note to Grandma with a handwritten sentiment and a decorated envelope. (Bottom)

- **Enlist your child's help** to create a "blank" album for a loved one who is battling an illness. The recipient's family members can add photos and journaling to the pre-decorated pages. (Below)

- **Ask children to help** decorate a "Love Notes" box where family members can leave kind notes and small treats for each other. (Opposite)

- **Enlist your child's help** in creating handmade "To/From" tags for plates of homemade cookies or other neighborly gifts.

- **Help your child** craft handmade thank-you cards to deliver upon receiving birthday or holiday gifts.

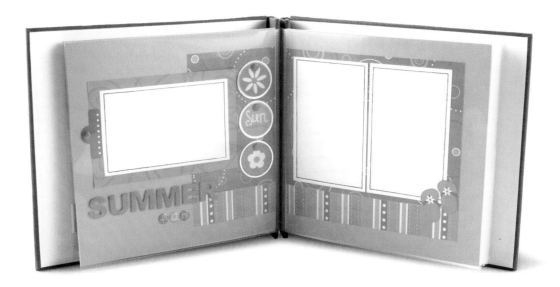

Spa party Set

"I think the *invitations* are soooooooooooooooooo cute!"

—MIRANDA W., AGE 10

You're Invited to a ...
Spa Party!

This tulip-themed spa party and matching party favors will make your party guests bubble up with joy. For a fun party activity, have guests give each other manicures on laminated placemats.

by Britney Mellen

chapter 4

parties

Give kids a *reason* to *celebrate* with a clever *art-inspired* approach to *everything* from gift *wrap* to *party* games.

project 1

by Jessie Baldwin

Round *out* your *projects* with *fun circle* shapes!

You Will Need: Cardstock, letter stickers, circle punches, inkpad, pen

Kid-Friendly: Have your child punch circles from cardstock and attach them to the background.

Variation

Use circle punches to create your own artwork, like the flower on this card.

Try This: Try cutting circles in half to make butterfly wings.

1

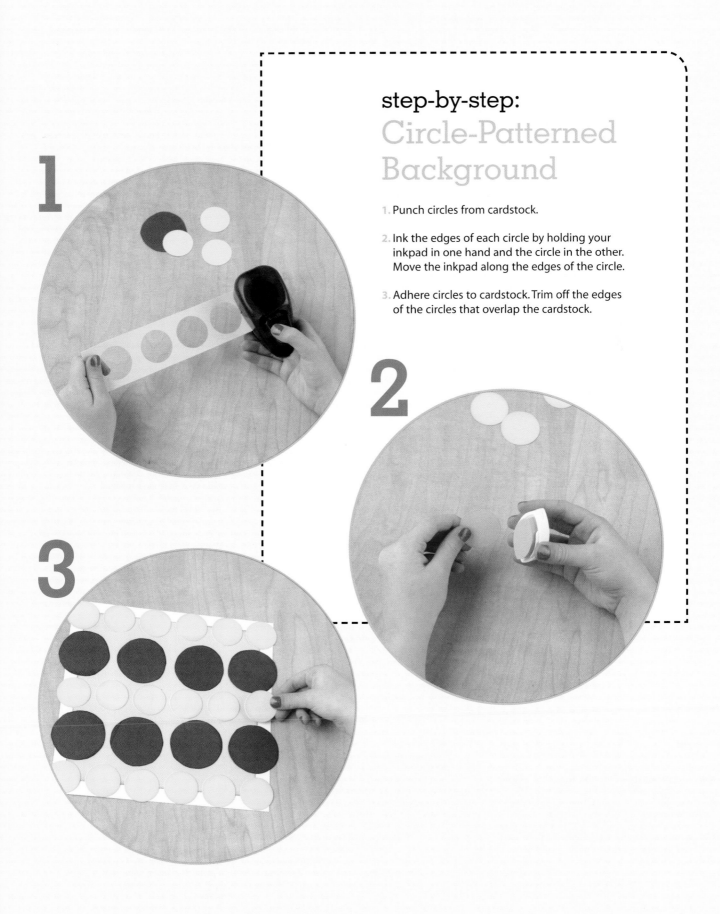

step-by-step:

Circle-Patterned Background

1. Punch circles from cardstock.

2. Ink the edges of each circle by holding your inkpad in one hand and the circle in the other. Move the inkpad along the edges of the circle.

3. Adhere circles to cardstock. Trim off the edges of the circles that overlap the cardstock.

2

3

project 2

by Marla Kress

Create a *surprise* party on your *page* with bright *colors!*

You Will Need: Cardstock, patterned paper, notebook paper, letter stickers, pen, number die cut

Kid-Friendly: Have your child handwrite her birthday highlights, and trace and cut numbers for the layout.

Variation

Use scraps from your scrapbook page to create a matching card.

Try This: Make a grid card. Divide your card into four sections and add one embellishment to each section.

1

step-by-step:
Birthday Layout

1. Gather page supplies. Cut patterned paper to size.

2. Add letter stickers to notebook paper to create the title.

3. Journal on the notebook paper, writing out both questions about the party and the child's answers.

4. Adhere all elements to cardstock and add a photo.

2

3

4

project 3

by Gail Robinson

Your *birthday's* the *center* of *attention* with this *army* theme.

You Will Need: Cardstock, phrases cut from patterned paper, journaling strips, photo corners

"I really like army stuff, and this was fun for my birthday." —DAVID R., age 9

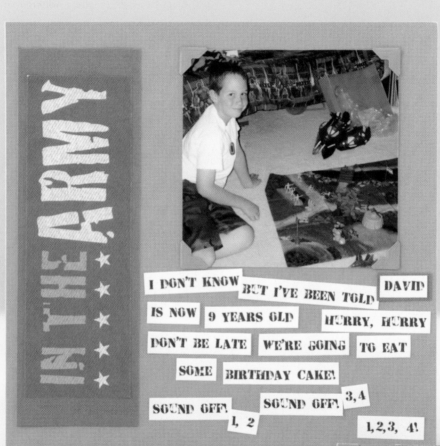

Variation

Use scraps to create an army-themed party invitation. Then invite your friends to a party they'll love!

Try This: Embellish a project with a favorite small toy.

1

step-by-step:
Army Birthday Layout

1. Cut phrases from patterned paper (or use cardstock stickers) and mat on cardstock. Adhere to page.

2. Crop your photo if needed. Adhere to page with photo corners.

3. Print or write additional journaling. Cut apart and attach to the layout as shown.

2

3

project 4

by Jessie Baldwin

Celebrate your party *memories* forever with this *cute* mini book!

You Will Need: Mini book, cardstock, letter stickers, decorative-edge scissors, inkpad

Kid-Friendly: Have your child design the book cover and embellish the pages.

Look inside!

Capture your favorite memories with photos that are important to you.

Try This: Create a mini book as a birthday gift for a friend!

step-by-step:
Mini-Book Cover

1. Trim the cardstock into squares, and the patterned paper into a strip.

2. Use decorative-edge scissors to make a wave edge on the largest piece of cardstock.

3. Ink the edges of the paper and layer them onto each other. Adhere to front of mini-book. Decorate as desired.

project 5

by Joannie McBride

by Joannie McBride

Wrap up your gifts in style!

You Will Need: Gift bag, patterned paper, inkpad

"This is so fast and easy, and I can do it!" —JOSIE R., age 7

Variation

Wrap up the fun with hand-stamped gift wrap.

Try This: Choose patterned papers that express the recipient's personality (for example, an apple print for a teacher or a princess print for a young girl).

1

2

3

step-by-step:
Decorated Gift Bag

1. Cut strips of patterned paper to size.

2. Ink the edges of the patterned paper.

3. Glue the strips of patterned paper to the bag.

project 6

by C. D. Muckosky

Tag, you're it! Add a *personal* touch to a *package* for a favorite *friend.*

You Will Need: Cardstock, patterned paper, flower stickers, string, beads, felt flower, rickrack, pen

Kid-Friendly: Have your child cut and decorate the tag.

Variation

Make tags in a variety of of shapes and sizes.

Try This: Look around your house for different shapes to trace. Cut out the traced images and turn them into an assortment of gift tags!

1

step-by-step:
Flower Gift Tag

1. Cut a tag from cardstock. Punch a hole in the top of the tag.

2. Decorate the tag with a pen. Add stickers if desired.

3. String beads onto thread.

4. Tie beads onto the tag. Add a felt flower and ribbon if desired.

2

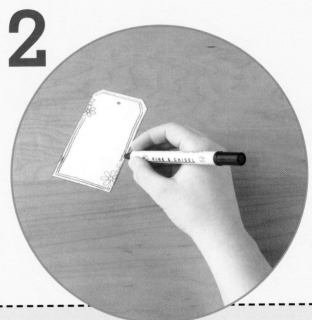

3

4

project 7

by Greta Hammond

Your *guests* will be the *center* of attention with these *fun* party *games!*

You Will Need: Cardstock, patterned paper, flower stamps, inkpad, circle punch

Play This: Make one set of matching cards for each party guest. Win the game by flipping over the most sets of matching cards.

Variation

Hit the bull's-eye with this fun party game!

Play This: Each guest gets a card with his picture on it. The guest who places his photo closest to the center of the board, with her eyes closed, wins!

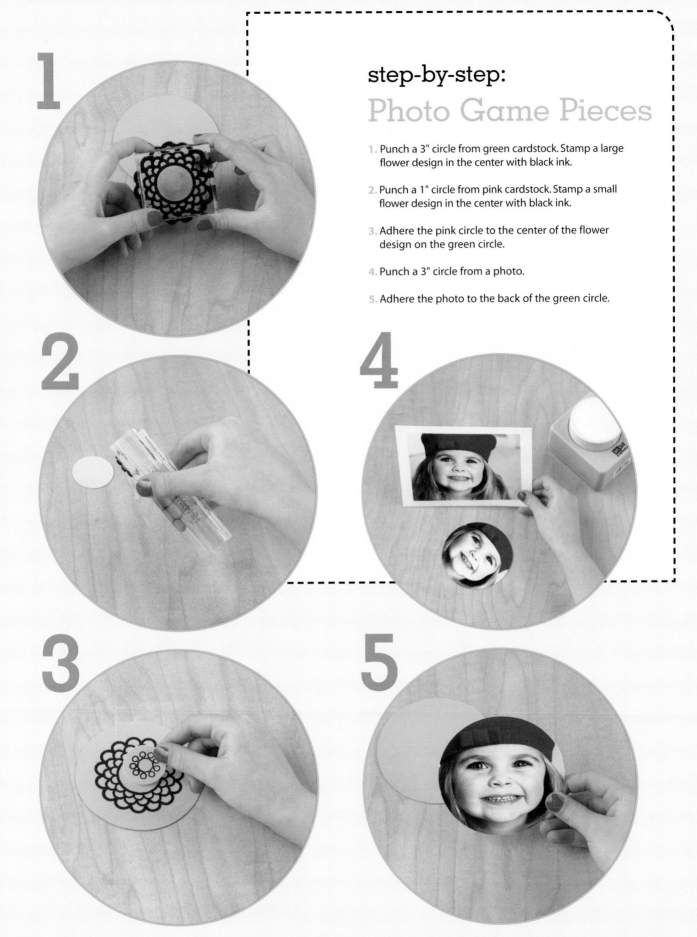

1

2

3

step-by-step:
Photo Game Pieces

1. Punch a 3" circle from green cardstock. Stamp a large flower design in the center with black ink.

2. Punch a 1" circle from pink cardstock. Stamp a small flower design in the center with black ink.

3. Adhere the pink circle to the center of the flower design on the green circle.

4. Punch a 3" circle from a photo.

5. Adhere the photo to the back of the green circle.

4

5

project 8

by Jessie Baldwin

Mix it up with this fun party game!

You Will Need: Cardstock, ruler, pencil, scissors
Play This: Deal cards and mix and match for silly combinations!

Variation

Have fun and create a whole variety of party games!

Play This: Mix and match photographs of pets with the corresponding letter of the alphabet.

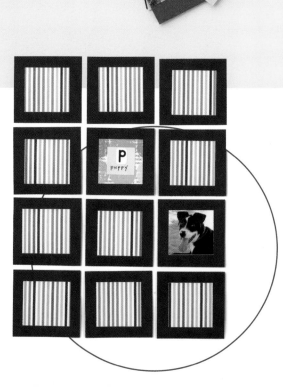

step-by-step:
Game Cards

1. Trim black and colored cardstock into 4" x 6" blocks. Glue together. The black cardstock will be the back of your cards.

2. Print a vertical 4" x 6" photo that shows a full-length body. Trim and adhere to colored cardstock.

3. Using a ruler, mark the cardstock at 2" and 4" with a pencil, then trim into three pieces. Repeat to create additional matching cards.

project 9

by Miriam Campbell

Add a little *flavor* to these *cool* party *favors!*

You Will Need: Lip balm in assorted colors, patterned paper, heart punch, ribbon

Kid-Friendly: Have your child wrap the tubes of lip balm with paper and add butterfly wings and ribbon.

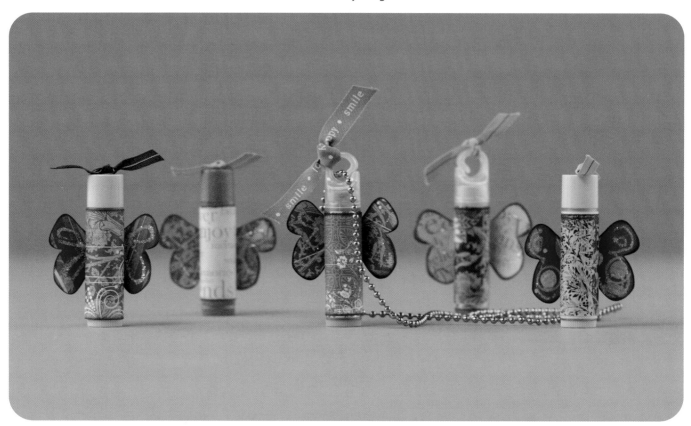

Variation

Match your party invitation to your party favors!

Try This: Create party favors with little bottles of nail polish or mini bottles of perfume.

1

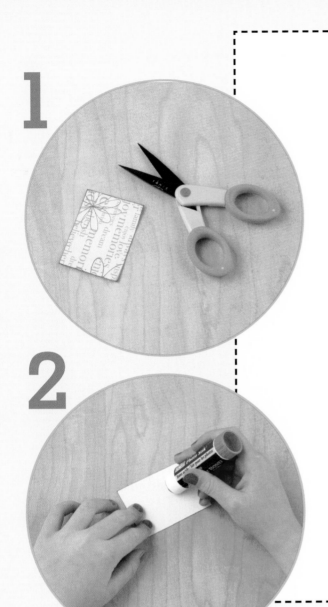

step-by-step:
Lip-Balm Butterfly

1. Cut patterned paper into a 1¾" x 2½" strip.

2. Apply glue to the back of the patterned paper.

3. Wrap the patterned paper around the lip-balm tube.

4. Punch two hearts from patterned paper to make butterfly wings.

5. Add glue to wings and attach to lip-balm tube.

2

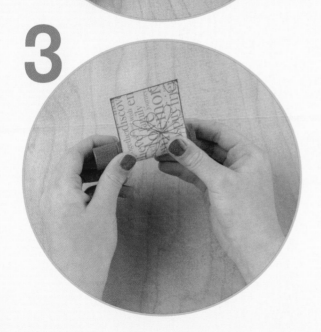

4

3

5

project 10

by Marla Kress

These *hanging* ribbon *frames* make great *party* favors!

You Will Need: Cardstock, patterned paper, ribbon, hole punch, corner-rounder punch, letter stickers, buttons
Kid-Friendly: Have your child weave ribbon onto the frame and embellish with buttons.

Variation

Alter the frame for a girl or a boy!

Try This: This is a great classroom project. Or, make these frames as gifts for family members!

1

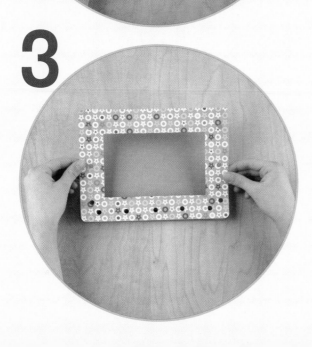

step-by-step:
Hanging Ribbon Frame

1. Trim one piece of patterned paper and one piece of cardstock into a 6" x 8" block. Round all of the corners. Hold papers together and punch holes evenly around the edges of three sides.

2. Cut a rectangle from the center of the patterned paper.

3. Put adhesive on the back of the bottom and sides of the patterned paper. Adhere to the cardstock, carefully lining up the holes.

4. Slide the picture into place. Glue top of frame closed.

5. Tie ribbon as shown and finish with embellishments.

2

4

3

5

project 11

by Erin Lincoln

Add a *bright* touch to your *next party* with this *adorable* felt garland.

You Will Need: Felt, ribbon, tags, craft knife, safety pin, letter stickers, buttons, heart punch

"I like the bright colors." —JAEME T., age 8

Variation

Create a whole set of matching decorations, including adorable felt hats.

Try This: Create a photo banner to decorate your bedroom!

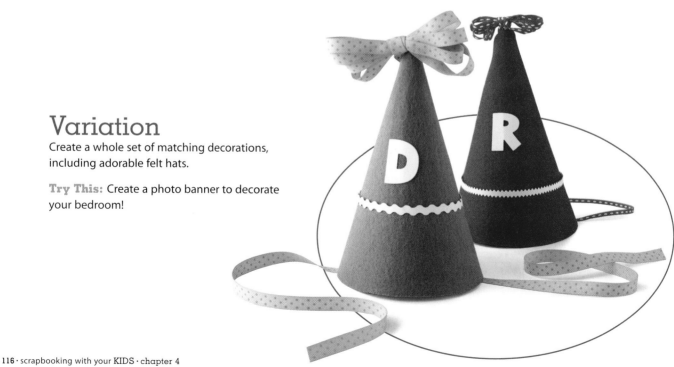

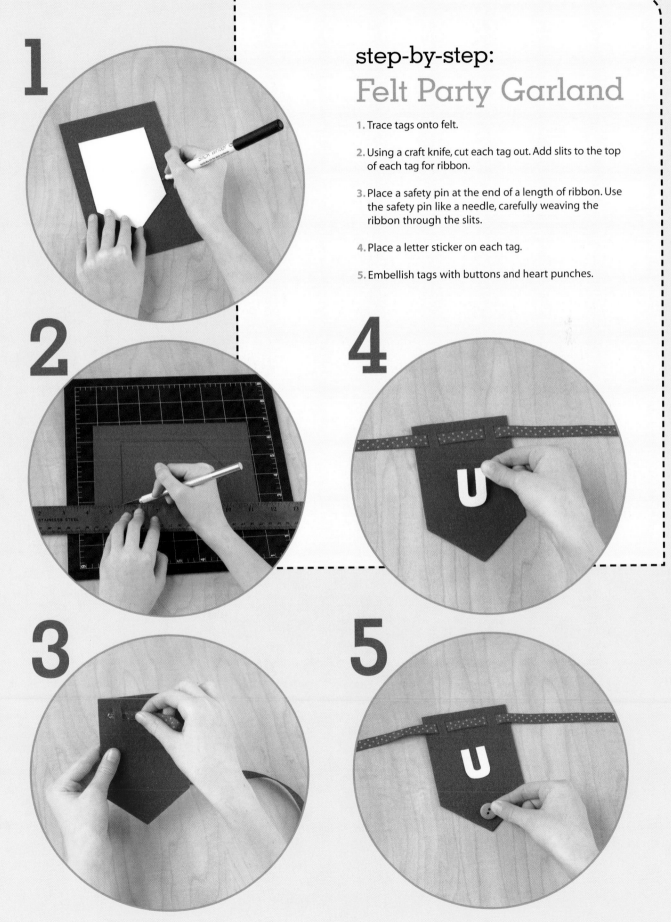

1

2

3

step-by-step:
Felt Party Garland

1. Trace tags onto felt.

2. Using a craft knife, cut each tag out. Add slits to the top of each tag for ribbon.

3. Place a safety pin at the end of a length of ribbon. Use the safety pin like a needle, carefully weaving the ribbon through the slits.

4. Place a letter sticker on each tag.

5. Embellish tags with buttons and heart punches.

4

5

article

Can you *share* some *fun ideas* for a
scrapbook-themed birthday *party*?

With a little preparation, scrapbooking can be a fun, stress-free party activity. The following five tips will help even the youngest guest grasp the basics of memory preservation:

- **Set out a "craft buffet"** with bowls of glitter, stickers, sequins and more, and let children customize framed photos of themselves. (Have a photo printer or Polaroid camera handy). (Opposite)

- **Have each child bring** a specific number of photos of an event. Provide premade layouts that each child can personalize with photos and decorations. (Bottom)

- **When hosting** any type of crafting activity for children, use a painter's drop cloth to protect the floor from stains and spills.

- **To prepare** for a scrapbooking birthday party, prepare precut photo mats and borders to make page assembly a cinch for kids.

- **Prepare fill-in-the-blank** word blocks to help children complete journaling for their scrapbook pages. (Right)

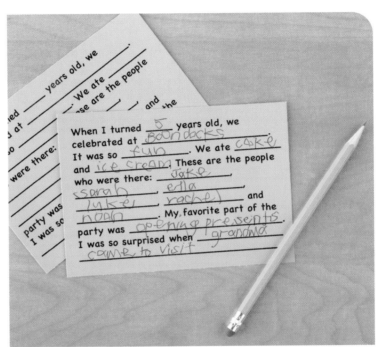

Purse Party Set

"I can't wait to give these to my friends! They're going to look so great in my room after my birthday party!" —MEAGAN A., AGE 9

You're Invited to ... a Purse Party!

by Wendy Sue Anderson

Want to throw a party that celebrates a pre-teen girl's fashionable purse-onality? Here's a fun way to do it, with invitations and favors that will help her remember her birthday in style!

"PURSE"-onal items for you!

You're invited

I would like to "PURSE"-onally invite you to my 10th birthday party!

saturday, June 17th
3:00 pm
at my house

please RSVP to my mom
by Friday {123-4567}

holidays

Pint-sized Picassos will enjoy a fresh spin on traditional holiday activities.

project 1

by Greta Hammond

Enjoy *Christmas* joy all *year round* with a *page* displaying Christmas *photos!*

You Will Need: Cardstock, patterned paper, buttons, foam letters, circle punch, double-sided tape, gold micro beads, button

"This is the most fun I've had in a lot of days!" —LIAM H., age 6

Variation

Mix patterned papers to create a joyful greeting card.

Try This: Experiment with different titles for a perfect fit.

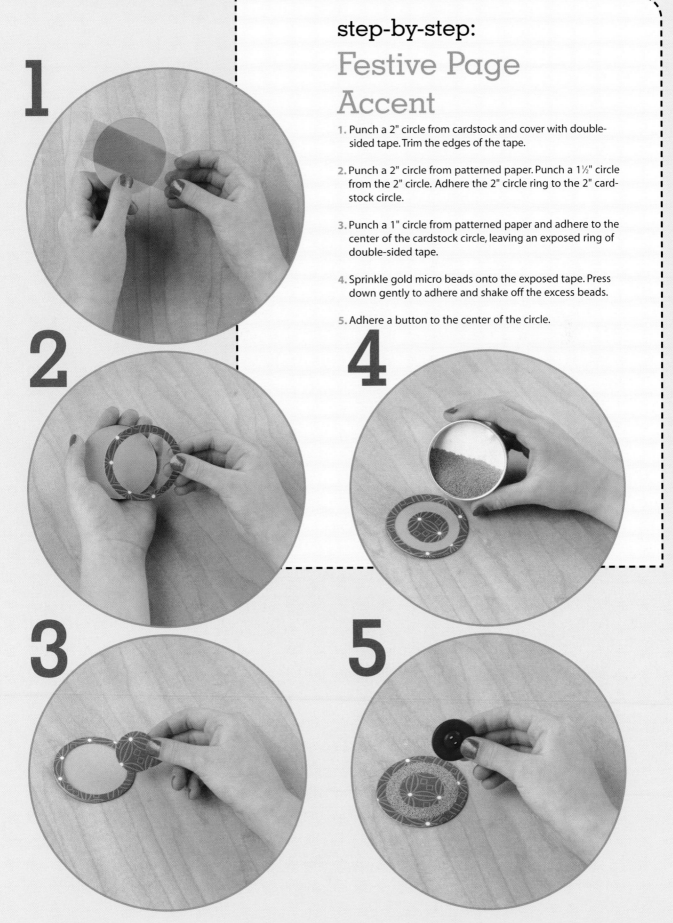

1

2

3

4

5

step-by-step:
Festive Page Accent

1. Punch a 2" circle from cardstock and cover with double-sided tape. Trim the edges of the tape.

2. Punch a 2" circle from patterned paper. Punch a 1½" circle from the 2" circle. Adhere the 2" circle ring to the 2" cardstock circle.

3. Punch a 1" circle from patterned paper and adhere to the center of the cardstock circle, leaving an exposed ring of double-sided tape.

4. Sprinkle gold micro beads onto the exposed tape. Press down gently to adhere and shake off the excess beads.

5. Adhere a button to the center of the circle.

project 2

by Vicki Harvey

Fall into the *season* with *autumnal paper* colors and a *golden* leaf!

You Will Need: Cardstock, patterned paper, ribbon, letter stickers and rub-ons, chipboard numbers, silk leaf, pen

"Can we use a real leaf???" —KENDALL H., age 6

Every year before Halloween we go to Berry Hill Farm in Anoka to get our pumpkins. I love this family tradition.

pumpkin **farm**

0 6

Variation

Send fall greetings with a handmade card.

Try This: Use small photo corners to accent patterned-paper corners.

happy **fall**

1

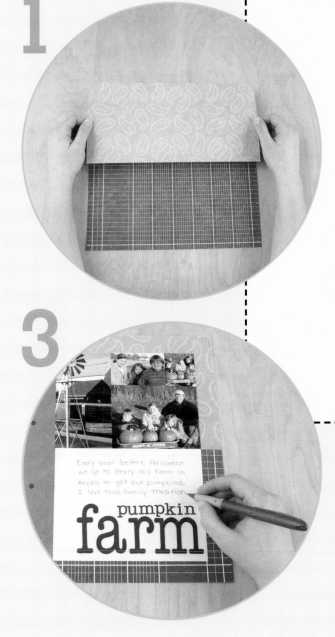

step-by-step:
Fall Days Layout

1. Layer half of the background paper with yellow paisley patterned paper.

2. Attach a strip of green paper and a block of ledger paper over the first layer. Add photos.

3. Add a title using letter stickers and rub-ons. Add journaling to the ledger paper.

4. Use ribbon to cover the seam between the green paper and the photos. Add a silk leaf, and add the date with chipboard numbers.

2

3

4

project 3

by Vicki Harvey

Adorn *your* layout with a *holly-berry* tag for *special* holiday *cheer!*

You Will Need: Cardstock, patterned paper, round metal-rimmed tag, ribbon, rub-on numbers, chipboard letters, small circle punch, small leaf punch, white pen

Kid-Friendly: Have your child journal on the black cardstock with a white pen and use the circle punch to create the holly-berry tag.

Grandpa and Jessica came up from Iowa to spend the Christmas holidays with us. We were blessed to spend time with family.

Variation

Swap the holly-berry tag for a floral print.

Try This: Mix paisley, floral, polka-dot and plaid patterns for visual interest.

step-by-step:
Holiday Layout

1. Layer green and red papers over the floral background.

2. Mat photos on black cardstock and journal directly on the black cardstock with a white gel pen.

3. Create an embellishment by adhering three small circles punched from red paper and two holly leaves punched from green paper to a metal-rimmed tag. Tie a bow onto the tag with ribbon.

4. Attach the embellished tag to the photo collage, and adhere the photo collage to the layout. Create a title with chipboard letters and rub-on numbers.

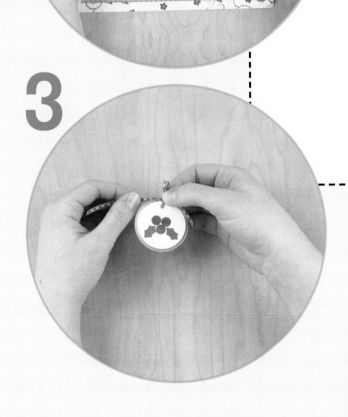

project 4

by Wendy Sue Anderson

Commemorate all of your family's annual *holidays* in one *festive mini* album!

You Will Need: Mini album, letter stickers, paper tags, ribbon, large number die cuts, stamps, inkpad, watercolor pencils, string

Kid-Friendly: Ask your children to record or discuss memories from each holiday. They can also color the stamped images on the tags.

Look Inside!

Use letter stickers, papers and photos to designate each holiday!

Try This: Create a mini album full of family birthday celebrations throughout the year.

1

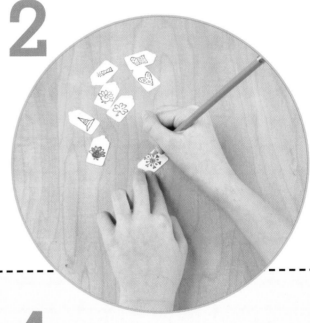

step-by-step:
Mini-Book Cover

1. Stamp a separate holiday-themed image onto each tag with dye-based ink.

2. Color the stamped images with watercolor pencils.

3. Use heavy string to tie the tags through the spine of the mini album.

4. Add a title with letter stickers and large number die cuts. Tie the mini book closed with ribbon.

2

3

4

Fashion **charming** *ornaments* in a few *simple* **steps.**

You Will Need: Cardstock, patterned paper, ribbon, metal beads, circle punches

Kid-Friendly: Have your child select the paper designs and punch the paper circles.

Variation

Create a holiday garland with various-sized ornaments.

Try This: Mix and match patterned papers and beads to create decorations for Easter, Halloween or Independence Day.

1

step-by-step:
Holiday Ornaments

1. Punch four 3" circles and four 2" circles from four different but coordinating patterned papers.

2. Adhere small circles to the centers of the larger circles. Fold the combined circles in half, creating a crease.

3. Adhere the flat edges of the two folded circles together. Repeat.

4. Put adhesive on the flat edges of the adhered folded circles. Loop a ribbon strip and place against the flat edge of a circle. Adhere both flat edges together, creating a sphere.

5. Add beads to both ends and tie a knot at the bottom.

2

4

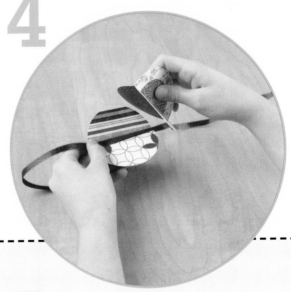

3

5

project 6

by Jessie Baldwin

Create a *whimsical* ornament *with colorful* curls of *paper*.

You Will Need: Construction paper, stapler, hole punch, scissors, pencil, ribbon
Kid-Friendly: Have your child select the paper and curl the paper strips.

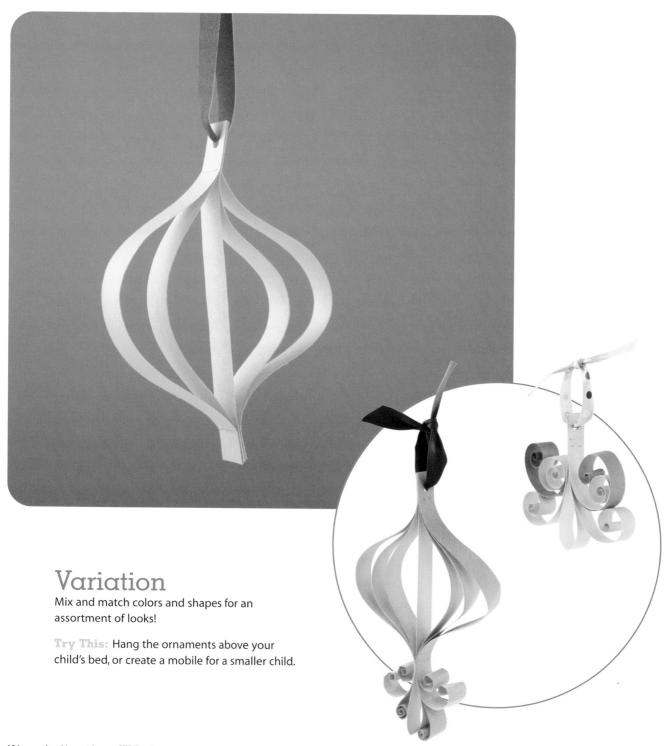

Variation

Mix and match colors and shapes for an assortment of looks!

Try This: Hang the ornaments above your child's bed, or create a mobile for a smaller child.

step-by-step:
Paper-Curl Ornament

1. Trim strips of construction paper to various lengths.

2. Staple the strips together, about 1" from the top.

3. Line up the bottom ends and staple together, about ½" from the bottom.

4. Punch a hole at the top and string a ribbon through the hole to hang the ornament.

project 7

by Denine Zielinski

Give and *receive* love *notes* in this cute *mailbox*!

You Will Need: Small metal mailbox, patterned paper, ruler, circle punch

"I'm so excited to have this for my school valentines!" —DEANNA T., age 9

Variation

Customize a mini mailbox for any holiday.

Try This: Raise the flag to notify your little one of a waiting treat or note!

1

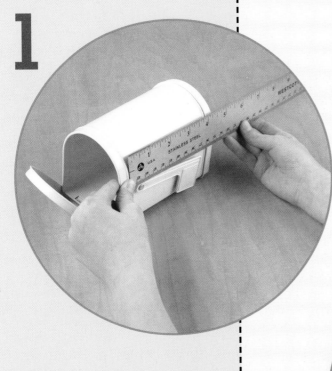

step-by-step:
Valentine Mailbox

1. Measure the mailbox to determine the correct proportions of patterned paper you'll need.

2. Cut patterned paper to correct size.

3. Decorate mailbox as desired.

2

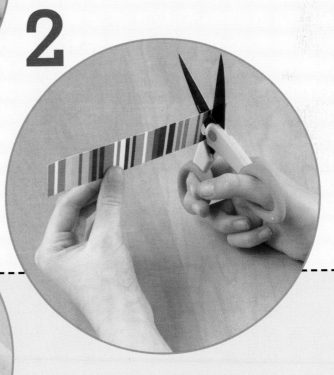

3

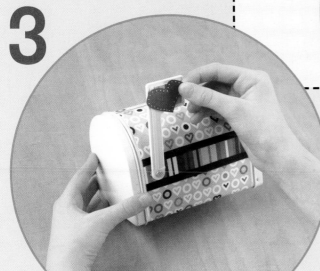

project 8

by Jessie Baldwin

A cute *bat* treat *bag* can *double* as a spooky *decoration*!

You Will Need: Construction paper or cardstock, stapler, circle punch, hole punch, ribbon

Kid-Friendly: Have your child make cone shapes with paper and choose the character details.

Variation

Create a silly, chilling or happy witch as an alternative to a bat!

Try This: Suspend the treat cones from a doorway as decorations.

step-by-step:
Bat-Shaped Treat Bag

1. Fold cardstock into a cone shape and staple.

2. Trim cardstock into wings and adhere to the back of the cone.

3. Use a circle punch to punch out eyes from yellow cardstock. Trim yellow cardstock as shown. Use a hole punch to make pupils for the eyes. Adhere.

4. Punch holes on each side of the cone and string ribbon through to make a handle.

project 9

by Linda Harrison

Cheery *bunnies* make *"hoppy"* napkin rings!

You Will Need: Cardstock, glitter, ribbon, patterned paper, pencil, pen

"My favorite part was making the glitter ears and picking out ribbon to tie for the bow." —SHANNON K., age 7

Variation

Slightly adjust the napkin rings to create cute egg holders.

Try This: Swap out the bunny shape for a chick, lamb or Easter egg!

1

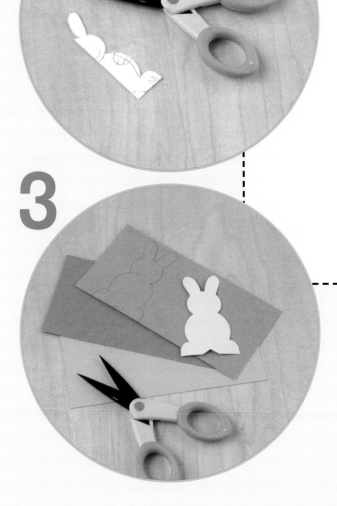

step-by-step:
Easter Bunny Napkin Rings

1. Create a bunny template by sketching a bunny and cutting it in half.

2. Fold a thick piece of cardstock in half and place the cut edge of the bunny template along the folded edge. Trace the pattern onto the cardstock.

3. Cut out the bunny template and unfold. Repeat as desired.

4. Embellish cardstock bunnies with glitter, ribbon and other embellishments. Attach a ring of patterned paper.

2

3

4

project 10

by Greta Hammond

Gobble, *gobble*! Designate the *place* settings for your *Thanksgiving feast* with a *cute* turkey place card!

You Will Need: Cardstock, patterned paper, scallop-edge scissors, circle punches, pen, dimensional adhesive

Kid-Friendly: Have your child punch cardstock circles, trace her fingers for turkey feathers and write guests' names on the place cards.

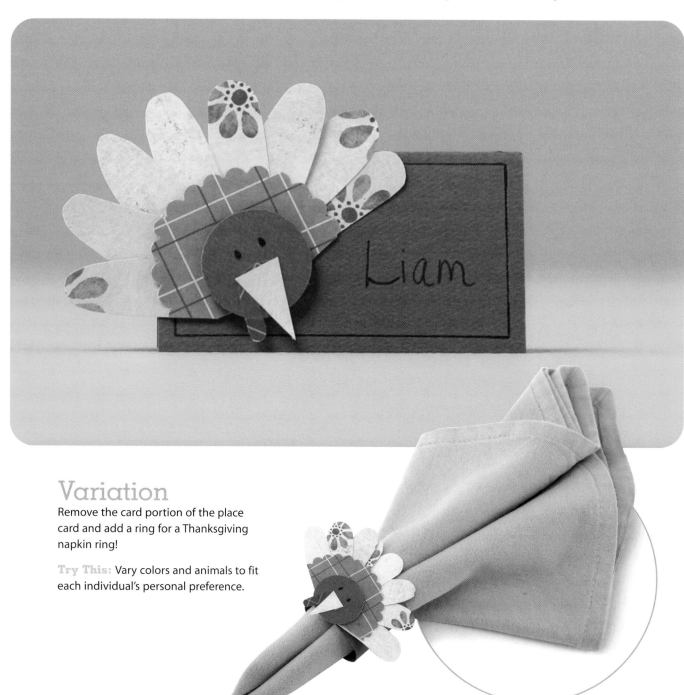

Variation

Remove the card portion of the place card and add a ring for a Thanksgiving napkin ring!

Try This: Vary colors and animals to fit each individual's personal preference.

1

step-by-step:
Turkey Accent

1. Trace a child's finger onto printed cardstock and cut enough to make eight feathers.

2. Punch a 2" circle from patterned paper. This will be the body of your turkey. Trim with scallop-edge scissors. Cut the bottom third of the circle away with a trimmer.

3. Using the scalloped edge as your base, fan out the feathers behind the circle and adhere.

4. Punch a 1" circle from brown cardstock. Draw eyes with a black pen, and cut and adhere a triangle beak and wattle.

5. Attach the turkey head to the body with dimensional adhesive.

2

4

3

5

project 11

by Emily Magleby

Craft an *ornament* that *sparkles* as brightly as the *smiles* on your *children's* faces!

You Will Need: Styrofoam balls, glitter, quilt pins with iridescent red and white heads, ribbon, circle punch

Kid-Friendly: Have your kids adhere glitter to the balls and attach the photos.

Variation

Assemble a cute snowman photo stand.

Try This: Flatten the bottom of the snowball photo ornament to create a gift-worthy picture frame.

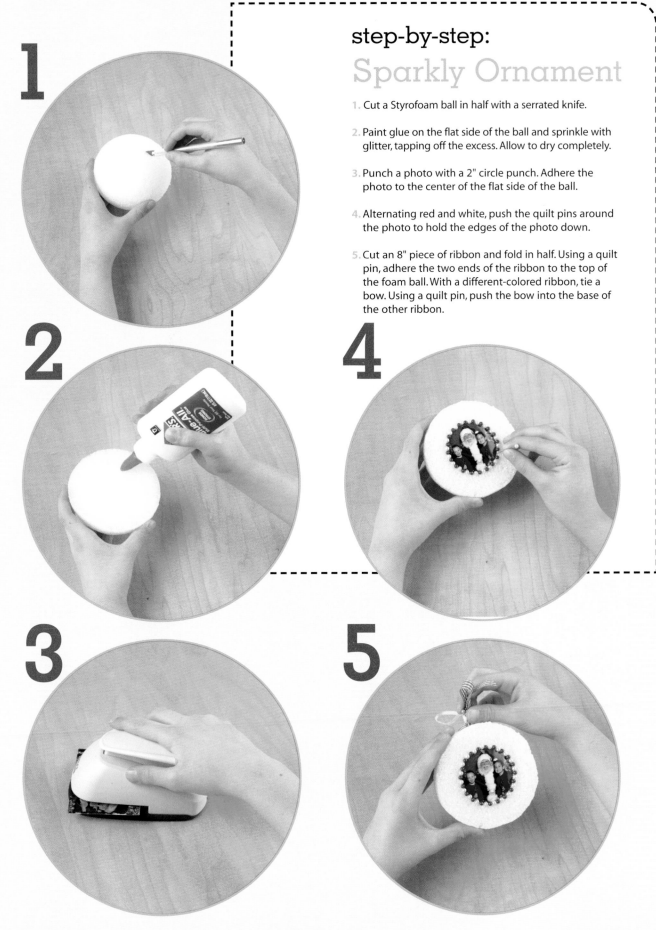

1

2

3

4

5

step-by-step:
Sparkly Ornament

1. Cut a Styrofoam ball in half with a serrated knife.

2. Paint glue on the flat side of the ball and sprinkle with glitter, tapping off the excess. Allow to dry completely.

3. Punch a photo with a 2" circle punch. Adhere the photo to the center of the flat side of the ball.

4. Alternating red and white, push the quilt pins around the photo to hold the edges of the photo down.

5. Cut an 8" piece of ribbon and fold in half. Using a quilt pin, adhere the two ends of the ribbon to the top of the foam ball. With a different-colored ribbon, tie a bow. Using a quilt pin, push the bow into the base of the other ribbon.

article

How can my child and I create with recycled items?

When in doubt, don't throw it out! Even the most ordinary items can ignite a child's imagination—prepare to be surprised! Follow these five tips to help turn that trash into treasure:

- **Use stencils and die cuts** to create interesting shapes out of old greeting cards. (Bottom)

- **Have children select** a worn-out book from their stash to convert into a mini album of favorite memories. (Right)

- **Keep empty ribbon spools** to use as templates for tracing perfect circles on art projects. (Opposite)

- **Save empty boxes**, string, bottle caps and other odds and ends that will provide endless hours of creative fun for children supplied with scissors and a glue stick!

- **Equip children** with a stack of old magazines, construction paper and a pair of scissors to create a picture-collage storybook.

Thanksgiving **party** Set

Please
Join Us

"I could *make* those name *cards* for *everyone* in our *family*. It would *give* me something to *do* when Mom is cooking the *turkey*." —BRANDON M., AGE 6

You're Invited to ....
a Thanksgiving Party!

by Vicki Harvey

The kids (and kids at heart) in your life will be thankful for this fun holiday party with a handmade theme! Just trace around a child's hand for the turkey feathers and embellish decorations and party favors as desired.

rainy days

Add these *innovative* boredom-*busters* to your *repertoire* and your *family* will actually look *forward* to the next rainy *day*!

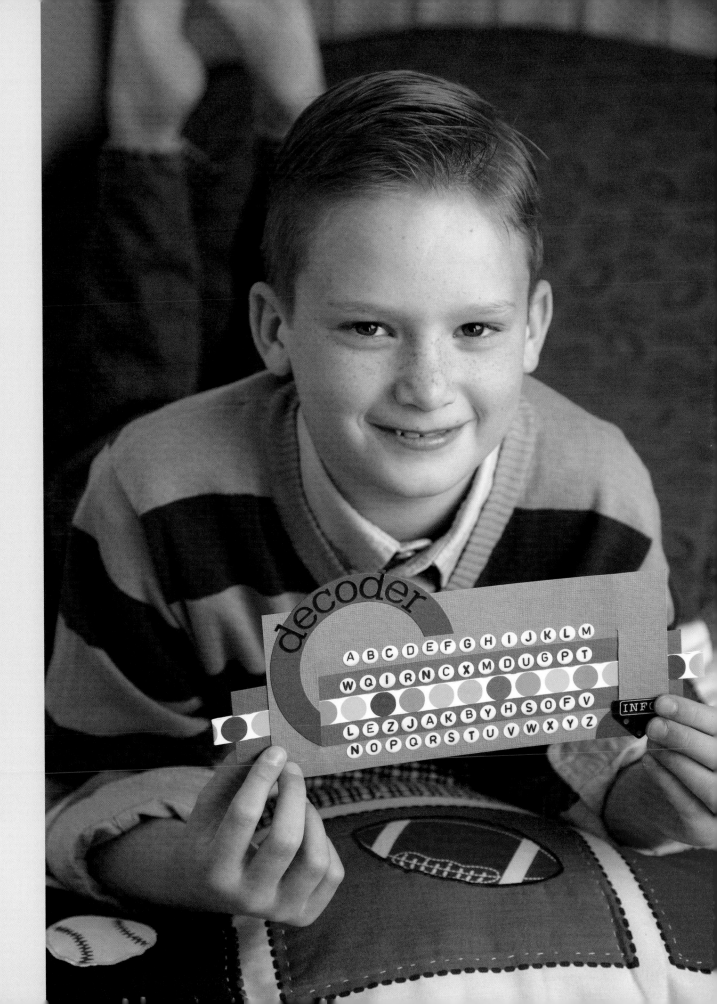

project 1

by Wendy Sue Anderson

Make a *splash* with this *rainy-day* page.

You Will Need: Cardstock, buttons, letter and number stickers

Kid-Friendly: Have your child choose the placement of the title, photos and buttons, and contribute a favorites checklist.

top 10 reasons to love a rainy day

the smell is so yummy!   everything is fresh and green

fun umbrellas   playing in puddles

staying cozy inside   watching the raindrops hit the window

playing in the rain   the smell (did i mention that?)

the contrast of colors   rainbows

Variation

A birthday card can be just as happy as an afternoon rain shower!

Try This: Brainstorm your top-ten list for other weather disruptions or seasons, such as summer, snowstorms or fall.

step-by-step:
Rainy-Day Page

1. Trim a sheet of green cardstock to 8" x 10". Then, print or handwrite your top-ten list on the green cardstock.

2. Create a photo collage and adhere on the left-hand side of the page.

3. Add a title with letter and number stickers.

4. Adhere the green cardstock to the red background and embellish with cardstock strips and buttons.

1

2

3

4

project 2

by Cindy Knowles

Post your *family* picture in a *place* *where* it's sure to be *seen*!

You Will Need: Clipboard, cardstock, patterned paper, rickrack, ribbon, letter stickers, brads, square punch, flower accents, stapler, photo corners

Kid-Friendly: Have your child place the title and rickrack on the page.

Variation

Creating a layout? Think about making a matching card or tag at the same time.

Try This: Instead of a one-photo clipboard, create a photo collage using school photos or family snapshots.

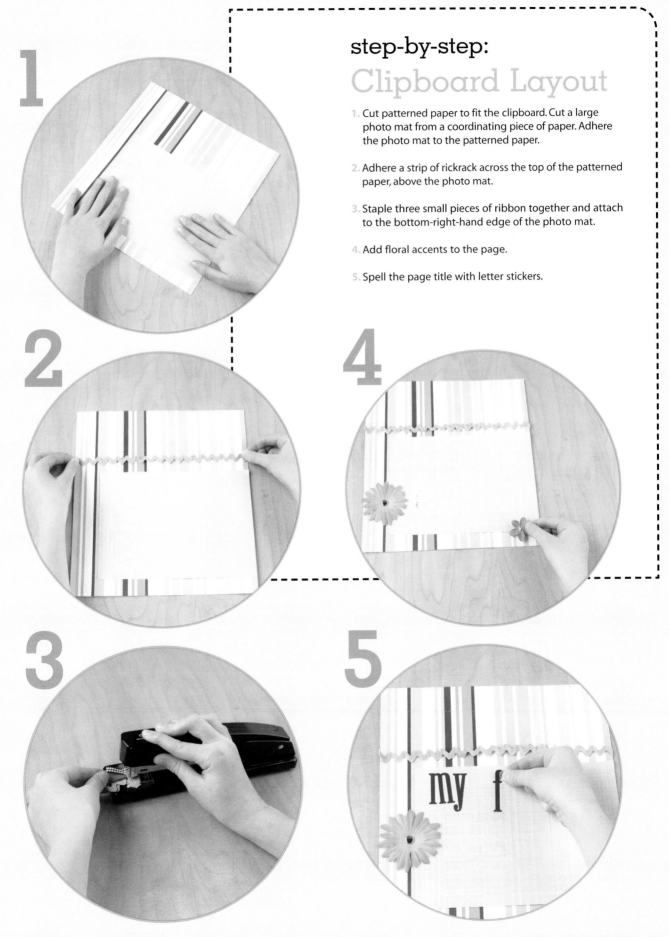

step-by-step:
Clipboard Layout

1. Cut patterned paper to fit the clipboard. Cut a large photo mat from a coordinating piece of paper. Adhere the photo mat to the patterned paper.

2. Adhere a strip of rickrack across the top of the patterned paper, above the photo mat.

3. Staple three small pieces of ribbon together and attach to the bottom-right-hand edge of the photo mat.

4. Add floral accents to the page.

5. Spell the page title with letter stickers.

Kick it up a *notch* with this *action-packed* soccer *page*!

You Will Need: Cardstock, patterned paper, ribbon
Kid-Friendly: Let your child pick out the ribbon scraps.

Variation

Help your soccer star create a sporty greeting card to share with her teammates.

Try This: Create a page or a card centered around any sport, such as softball, swimming or gymnastics.

1

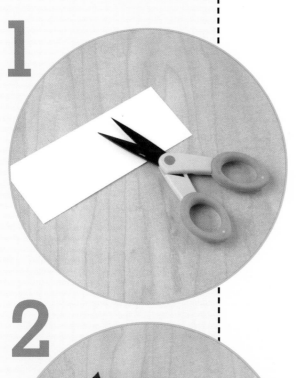

step-by-step:
Ribbon Accent

1. Cut a strip of cardstock to use for the base of the accent.

2. Choose an assortment of ribbons.

3. Cover cardstock with a thin layer of glue. Attach ribbons.

4. Trim off ends of the ribbons.

5. Place accent on layout as shown.

2

4

3

5

project 4

by Gail Robinson

Create a clever state-shaped mini book!

You Will Need: Chipboard, cardstock, patterned paper, chipboard letters, rickrack, letter stickers, hole punch, binder ring

Kid-Friendly: Have your child search for facts and interesting tidbits about your state.

Look inside!

Fill your book with fun state facts.

Try This: Visit places of interest within your state. Gather mementos, photos and memorabilia for your book!

1

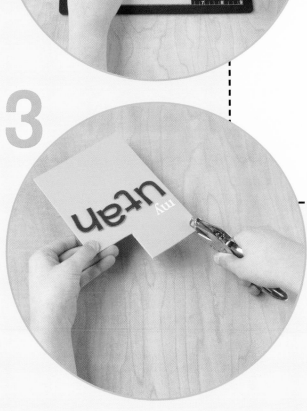

step-by-step:
State Mini-Book Cover

1. Cut a 1½" x 2" rectangle of chipboard using a sharp blade and cutting mat. Repeat for the back cover.

2. Decorate the front cover using chipboard letters and letter stickers.

3. Punch a hole in the top-left corner of the front and back cover.

4. Add embellishments and place a binder ring through the holes.

2

3

4

project 5

by Linda Harrison

What's the *secret* code? *Find* out *with* this special *project*!

You Will Need: Cardstock, letter stickers, pencil, scissors

"I liked being able to mix up the letter stickers to make my own code."
—ADAM W., age 8

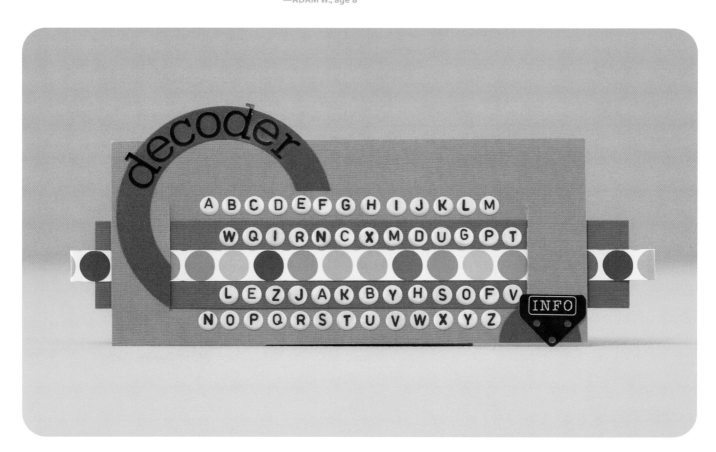

Variation

Vary colors, lettering and embellishments for a new look!

Just for Fun: Experiment with shapes and sizes for a more custom look.

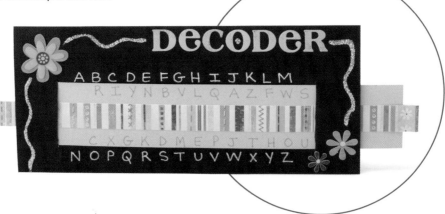

1

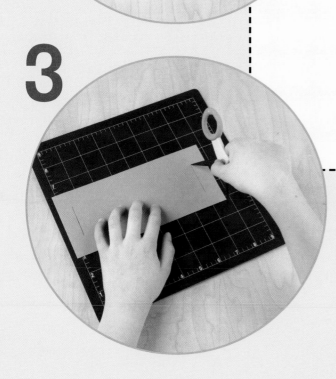

step-by-step:
Secret Decoder

1. Cut a piece of cardstock to 3½" x 8" to create the base. Cut a piece of cardstock to 1½" x 9" to create the slide.

2. Using the slide as a guide, mark pencil lines onto the base cardstock, approximately ¾" from each end of the base.

3. Using scissors, score and cut along the pencil lines.

4. Fit the slider piece of cardstock into the slits. Add letter stickers to the front of the decoder.

2

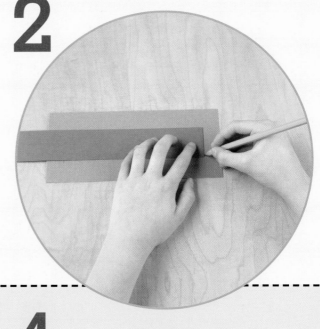

3

4

project 6

by C. D. Muckosky

Send some rainy-day cheer with this happy card!

You Will Need: Cardstock, stamp, inkpad, ribbon/yarn, mini tag punch, stapler, chalk, cotton swab

Kid-Friendly: Have your child stamp an image and write a message inside the card.

Variation

Make several greeting cards or tags to have on hand for any occasion!

Try This: Brush an inkpad along the edges of the card for a distressed, detailed look.

1

step-by-step:
Happy Card

1. Cut a small rectangle of cardstock and fold into a card. Punch a mini tag from white cardstock.

2. Stamp or cut designs onto cardstock to create the background.

3. Edge the mini tag with an inkpad, then stamp the image.

4. Color the stamped image with chalk or colored pencils.

5. Staple the mini tag to the card and add ribbon.

2

4

3

5

project 7

by C. D. Muckosky

Make your artwork *travel*-friendly with this cute *mini* album!

You Will Need: Cardstock, embroidery floss, stickers, colored pencils, white paper

Kid-Friendly: Have your child place the stickers and decorate the cover.

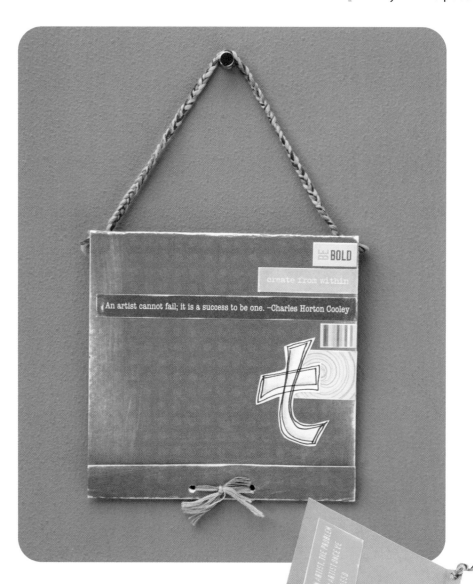

Look inside!

Fill the art book with sheets of blank paper for a ready-made art companion.

Try This: Mix and match materials for the handle.

1

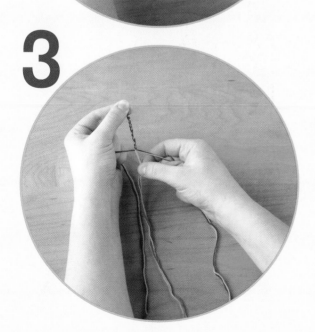

step-by-step:
Mini Art Album

1. Cut a piece of two-sided cardstock and fold.

2. Add white paper pages to the notebook and punch two holes through the bottom of the notebook (and the white pages).

3. Braid embroidery floss and tie through holes to create a handle.

4. Decorate the cover with stickers.

5. Draw pictures inside the notebook.

2

4

3

5

project 8

by Cindy Knowles

Play your *cards* right with these *personalized* playing cards! *Play* memory, Go Fish or other *pairing games* with the *cards*.

You Will Need: Playing cards, letter stamps, inkpad, letter stickers
Kid-Friendly: Have your child select the photos and glue them to the cards.

Variation

Add "all about me" cards to the mix!

Try This: Make playing cards with photos of animals or objects.

1

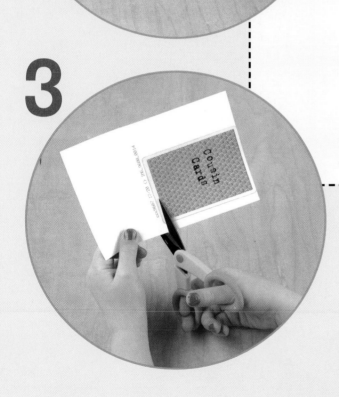

step-by-step:
Cousin Cards

1. Stamp "Cousin Cards" on the back of each playing card. (Each individual photo will need two playing cards.)

2. Apply glue to the face of the card and adhere the photo.

3. Allow glue to dry and trim away photo excess using the card edge as a guide.

4. Spell the first name of each cousin on each card with letter stickers.

2

3

4

Hide your special *treasures* in this *handmade* box.

You Will Need: Small chipboard or papier-mâché box, patterned paper, rickrack, decorative-edge scissors, heart punch

"I love that it's pink!" —VIOLET B., age 6

Variation

Create a box suited for all personalities using different colors and patterns.

Try This: Add a special touch with strips of pretty ribbon, buttons or decorative rub-ons.

step-by-step:
Treasure Box

1. Trim patterned paper slightly larger than the box top. Adhere to the top of the box.

2. Trim the corners of the paper, fold them over and adhere to the sides of the box top.

3. Glue rickrack around the edges of the box top.

4. Cut a strip of patterned paper to wrap around the bottom of the box. Finish the remaining flap of patterned paper by cutting with decorative-edge scissors. Adhere.

1

2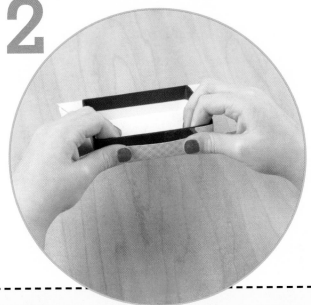

3

4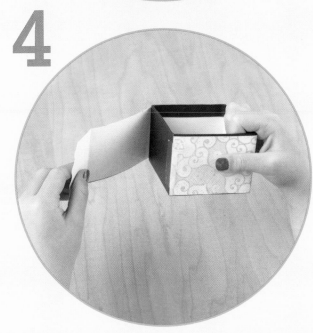

project 10

by Joannie McBride

Fill a *rainy* afternoon with suspenseful *adventure* using *clues* and a *treasure* map!

You Will Need: Cardstock, patterned paper, stapler, stickers, letter stickers, pen

Kid-Friendly: Have your child place treasure-map icons on the map.

Variation

Send a mini treasure quest to a friend as a card!

Try This: Have a treasure-map party!

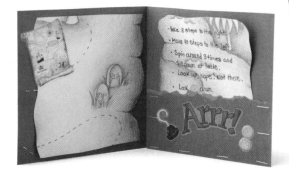

1

step-by-step:
Treasure Map and Clues

1. To create a treasure map, crinkle patterned paper and adhere to a 12" x 12" sheet of cardstock.

2. Staple along the edges. Add stickers.

3. To create game cards, cut two different shades of brown cardstock into shapes. Tear edges of the lighter cardstock.

4. Adhere the lighter cardstock to the dark cardstock. Add stickers and write instructions for the treasure hunt.

2

3

4

project 11

by Erin Lincoln

Allow your little *ones* to express themselves *with* this emotion *meter*!

You Will Need: Cardstock, crayons, letter stamps, label stamp, inkpad, letter stickers, circle punches, magnets

Kid-Friendly: Have your child punch circles from cardstock and draw facial expressions on them.

Variation

These cute little cubes will allow your child to show you how he's feeling each day!

Try This: Create a cube filled with your child's artwork.

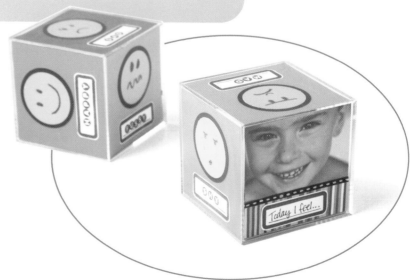

1

2

3

step-by-step:
Emotion Meter Magnets

1. Punch a circle from yellow cardstock.

2. Punch a larger circle from black cardstock.

3. Glue the yellow circle on top of the black circle. Use a black crayon to draw a facial expression.

4. Stamp a label on white cardstock and use letter stamps to label the emotion. Cut out

5. Glue the top edge of the label to the back bottom of the smiley face. Adhere a magnet to the back.

4

5

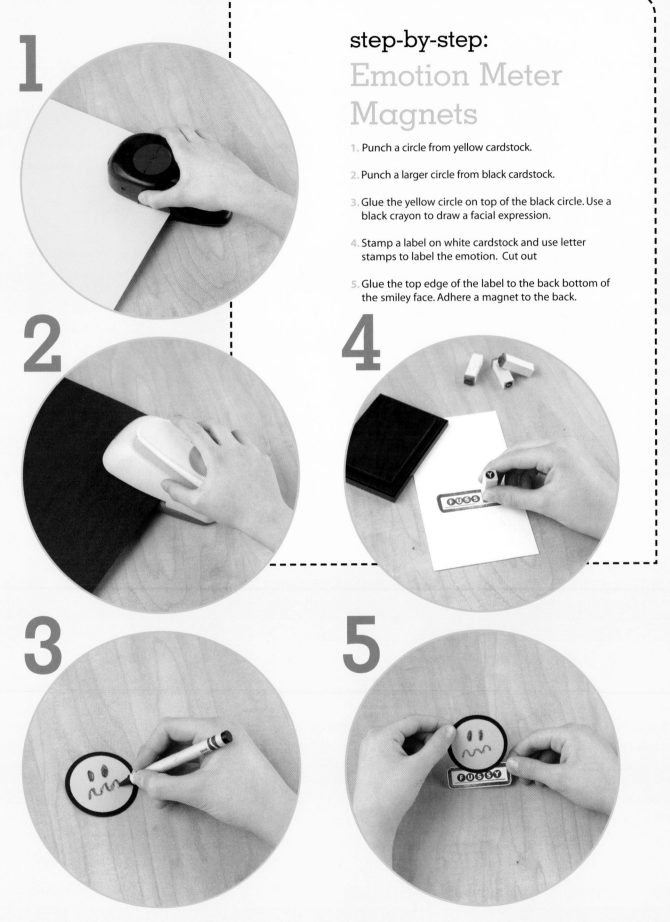

article

How can I *foster* my child's *creativity*?

Even more important than the right crafting space and supplies is a creative atmosphere, where children can feel free to express themselves. Try these five tips to help ignite young minds with a zeal for creating:

- **Rotate your child's art supplies** on a regular basis to promote creativity (and prevent boredom!).

- **Foster young imaginations** with open-ended questions, such as, "Tell me about what you've made," rather than, "What is that a picture of?"

- **Create a small album** of 10–20 sheets, each with a single graphic element somewhere on the page. Ask your child to incorporate the shapes as she "finishes" each page. (Bottom)

- **Pull out the paint**, chalk, crayons and markers and help your child experiment on new artistic canvases. Try the sidewalk, a chalkboard, rocks, an inexpensive glass mirror or a dry-erase board. (Right)

- **Prepare small creativity kits** to entertain young children in the car or at a restaurant. Include non-messy art supplies such as colored pencils, stickers and stencils. (Opposite)

and went up in a hot air balloon that was very colorful...

Ladybug party Set

"These are so *adorable*. I just *love* them! I really *like* the *party-favor* bag!" —KIMBERLY M., AGE 8

You're Invited to ... a Ladybug Party!

by Vicki Harvey

When it's rainy outside, bring the party inside with this adorable ladybug party set. Serve hot cocoa and cookies, play favorite games and enjoy the fun of a cozy day inside!

Please Join Us at Kendall's House March 21, 2007 1:00 pm-3:00pm RSVP - 391-7664

parents' guide

Learn the *best* **ways** to *inspire* *your* **young** *artists*.

parents' guide

Children of all ages love *sinking* their hands into *paint*, coloring with a box of brand-new crayons or *smearing* decoupage medium over a project. Adults like to *share* in the fun too! To help you achieve an experience that *fills* your child with a *sense* of accomplishment and grants you a sense of *fulfillment* (rather than frustration!), check out the following *guidelines* for *working* with children of varying age groups. The tips and *suggestions* will help you *plan* age-appropriate activities, creating a fun and stress-free *experience* for both of you—just what creating *art* should be!

a few basics

- Be sensitive to your child's need for your approval.

- Always accept and praise your child's creative efforts with positive feedback.

- Encourage your child's involvement, but never demand it. Don't scold him if his attention wanes or he loses interest.

- Remember, every child is different, and your child's skill set may differ from those listed in each category. Plan projects according to your child's capabilities and interests.

- Collect the necessary supplies for the project before beginning.

preschool (3–5)

Children within this age group are sharpening their fine motor skills, such as the ability to grasp, squeeze, rotate and pinch. They are extremely active but still uncoordinated and awkward. The younger children in this group are still developing their language skills, while the older children are beginning to recognize letters, numbers and words. Children this age are not yet skilled at problem-solving. Be patient with their inability to independently complete a project.

- **Plan activities** that are simple, direct and easy to finish. Children this age have extremely short attention spans.

- **Use artwork** as a way for your child to express her feelings. She can already associate colors with certain emotions.

- **Incorporate handwriting** or a picture your child has drawn into the project. Most of his art projects are unplanned, meaning he hasn't mapped out the end result before beginning. Allow for this in the overall project.

- **Assign simple tasks** and responsibilities for the project, such as coloring a shape, punching shapes from cardstock or matching colors.

- **Provide your child** with one task at a time, waiting until he has completed it before giving him another. Be cautious of overwhelming your child with too many complex instructions.

- **Limit your child's** choices, as her decision-making skills are still undeveloped. For instance, if you allow her to select a sheet of cardstock, give her only three or four options.

- **A simple mobile** is a great project for a child this age because it allows him to put his knowledge of basic art techniques to the test.

- **Consider visiting** a museum or looking through a book of paintings with your child. A child this age is capable of drawing simple observations about art (such as what she likes/dislikes or how the piece makes her feel).

- **With close supervision**, some children in this age group can begin to cut simple shapes and paste.

memories:

preschool

HARRY AGE 9 (four)

preschool was such a great experience for Harrison. He attended three days a week and just loved his teacher and classmates. (2005)

I miss you

Preschool Memories
I Miss You Card

by Harry and Kim Kesti.

k–3 (6–8)

During this age range, children begin to lengthen their attention span, but they still become restless and fidgety. Their logic and reasoning skills are developing, and while they might enjoy a challenge, a seemingly impossible task will frustrate them. They're still developing muscular control. They're often indecisive. They're becoming more aware of self and how they interact with the world. Most children this age can read.

- **Consider breaking** the project into a series of steps and allowing the child a break to stretch or have active play.

- **Avoid drawing attention** to his awkwardness. It's paramount for him to feel secure and unthreatened; be sure you don't discourage his creative efforts.

- **Allow the child** to make basic decisions about how the project will progress, but don't pose ambiguous questions such as, "What project shall we create?"

- **Encourage your child** to express her feelings through the project.

- **Help your child** set realistic goals and make some decisions. (The younger child in this group wants very much to be involved but may not be able to handle making many decisions. Give him small, simple tasks.)

- **Teach new concepts** in clear language with concrete examples.

- **Satisfy her craving** for hands-on involvement by allowing her to help with adhesive or project assembly.

- **Ask him to measure** accuracy with a ruler. Using an adult-size ruler makes him feel very important!

- **Allow your child** enough time to fully complete a task. This is extremely important to him.

Sophie has such a sunny personality that it's no surprise when her art subjects include flowers, trees and rainbows. At age seven, she is quite the artist. And, most of her artwork looks ready to...

{bloom}

BE HAPPY EVERY DAY

Bloom
Be Happy Every Day Card

by Sophie and Kim Kesti.

pre-teen (9–12)

Pre-teens have developed good body control and enjoy more complicated crafts and handiwork. They can handle a great deal of creative autonomy and decision-making. Children this age can be expected to maintain attention for a significant length of time. Girls tend to be more interested in design, while boys like to play with the art tools.

- **Help your child** decide on a project and allow her to choose colors and accents as well as where items will be placed.

- **Pre-teens enjoy** collecting, so consider a project that involves displaying or cataloging a collection.

- **Consider a project** that deals with the past and present as well as different cultures. These topics are of great interest to this age group.

- **Respect your child's** individual differences when completing projects.

- **Provide opportunities** for reading, writing and journaling. Children this age have great imaginations.

- **Remember, your child** is establishing her independence. She doesn't want to be treated like a child.

- **Show confidence** in his abilities and give praise for good behavior.

- **Ask for your child's** opinion on certain decisions and allow her to follow through. This creates a sense of ownership and responsibility.

- **If something goes wrong** with the project, don't take over. This is a time for learning, not for perfection.

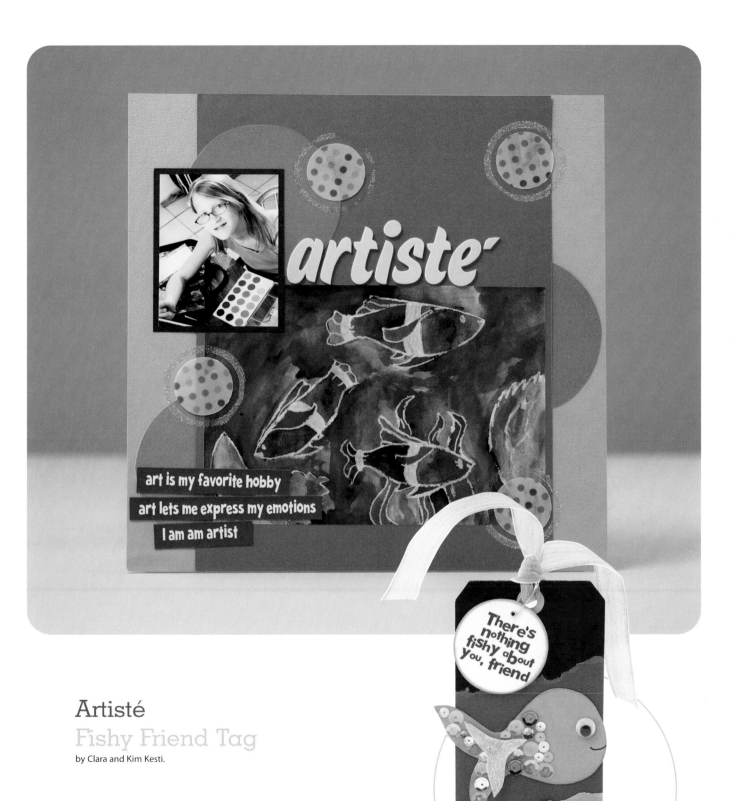

art is my favorite hobby

art lets me express my emotions

I am am artist

There's nothing fishy about you, friend

Artisté
Fishy Friend Tag

by Clara and Kim Kesti.

Fun Finder

Looking for something fun to do?
Try one of these great activities!

foreword

chapter 1: summer

chapter 2: school

chapter 3: gifts

chapter 4: parties

chapter 5: holidays

chapter 6: rainy days

A Special Thanks To:

Connor, age 10

Eliza, age 9

Whitney, age 8

Mia, age 6

Katherine, age 6

Hailey, age 5

Isaac, age 4

Ellie, age 3